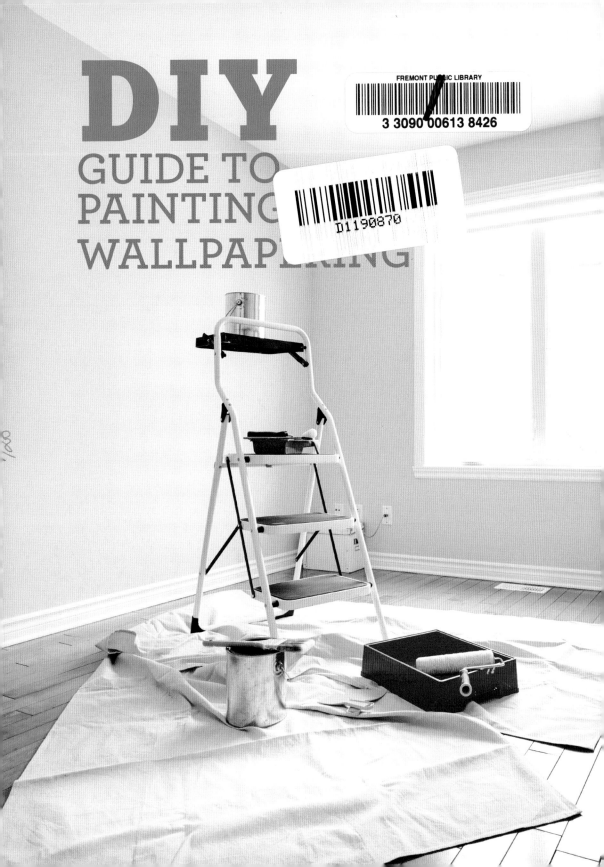

DIY

GUIDE TO
PAINTING
WALLPAPERING

CRE🏠TIVE
HOMEOWNER®

Copyright © 2010, 2018 Michael R. Light and Creative Homeowner

DIY Guide to Painting and Wallpapering (ISBN 978-1-58011-805-7) is a revised edition of *The DIY Decorator's Handbook* (ISBN 978-1-84773-422-8).

DIY Guide to Painting and Wallpapering
Vice President-Content: Christopher Reggio
Editor: Anthony Regolino
Technical Editor: Chris Cavanaugh
Copy Editor: Laura Taylor
Cover and Page Designer: Mary Ann Kahn
Indexer: Elizabeth Walker

ISBN 978-1-58011-805-7

Library of Congress Cataloging-in-Publication Data
Names: Light, M. R. (Michael R.), author.
Title: DIY guide to painting and wallpapering / Michael R. Light.
Description: Mount Joy, PA : Creative Homeowner, 2018. | Includes index.
Identifiers: LCCN 2017059793 | ISBN 9781580118057
Subjects: LCSH: Interior painting--Amateurs' manuals. |
   Paperhanging--Amateurs' manuals.
Classification: LCC TT323 .L54 2018 | DDC 747/.3--dc23
LC record available at https://lccn.loc.gov/2017059793

We are always looking for talented authors.
To submit an idea, please send a brief inquiry to acquisitions@foxchapelpublishing.com.

Printed in Singapore

Current Printing (last digit)
10 9 8 7 6 5 4 3 2 1

Creative Homeowner®, *www.creativehomeowner.com*, is an imprint of New Design Originals Corporation and distributed exclusively in North America by Fox Chapel Publishing Company, Inc., 800-457-9112, 903 Square Street, Mount Joy, PA 17552, and in the United Kingdom by Grantham Book Service, Trent Road, Grantham, Lincolnshire, NG31 7XQ.

DIY
GUIDE TO
PAINTING AND
WALLPAPERING

Michael R. Light

A Complete Handbook to Finishing
Walls and Trim for a Stylish Home

CRE▲TIVE
HOMEOWNER®
CreativeHomeowner.com

Contents

Introduction

When a friend of mine recently became a first-time home buyer, he wanted to know how to decorate his newly acquired property. He looked in bookshops and libraries for a small, informative book, only to find that most decorating books were tomes: thick books that covered many aspects of DIY, but only had a small section on decorating. They were, as he put it, "books to make your arms ache."

He knew that I had over 40 years of professional decorating experience and at one time had been a qualified technical instructor of painting and decorating, so he suggested that I write a small book on the subject, using my knowledge and experience of the trade.

Before I actually started to write, I did some research into the books that were currently available. I did, in fact, find that most were large, heavy books, with a few exceptions. These books, although smaller and containing lots of information, were what I would describe as piecemeal, a bit of this and a bit of that with little continuity of the subject. So what I have tried to present here is a dedicated decorating book, set out in a progressive and step-by-step format. The text not only tells you what to do, but the illustrations show you how to go about doing it.

The book is intended to give professional decorating advice to anyone who is prepared to tackle the job for him- or herself, particularly the first-time DIY decorator. The main aspects of decorating work are covered, including preparation of surfaces, with many types of materials outlined. Faults and problems with paint finishes and wallpaper are described with remedies and solutions listed, and types of tools and brushes used are illustrated. Throughout the book there are dozens of "decorator's dodges"—shortcuts and useful hints to save you time and effort.

I hope that the information I've provided will be useful to you and that my knowledge of the industry will encourage you to tackle your decorating work. There is no better teacher than experience, which with the help of this book you will gain.

How to Use
This Book

This book is intended to give professional decorating advice to anyone who is prepared to tackle the job on his or her own, in particular, the first-time DIY decorator. The main aspects of decorating work are covered and many types of materials are described.

Not only does it tell you what to do, but shows you, with the help of hundreds of diagrams, many of which provide you with step-by-step instructions. Throughout the book dozens of decorator's dodges are described—look for these for useful shortcuts, hints, and tips.

The book is divided into four main sections: Before You Begin; Preparation; Painting; and Hanging Wallpaper. A detailed index makes it easy for you to find what you want quickly.

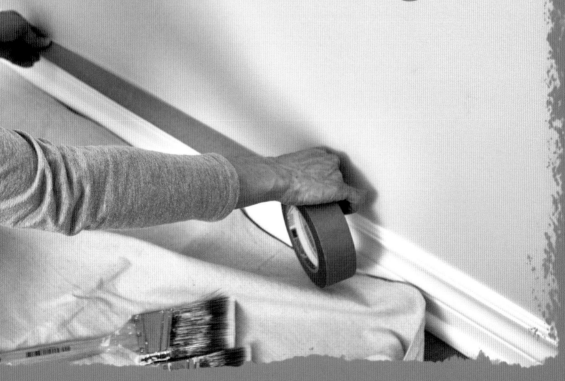

Part One

Before You Begin

Basic Requirements for Starting

Ladders and stepladders are basic to many DIY decorating projects, and wooden planks also have a role to play in some circumstances.

General painting You will need a stepladder. Note that ceilings can be painted using a roller on an extension pole handle, so you may only need to use the stepladder for cutting in the edges of the ceiling.

Painting ceilings You will need two stepladders and a plank. Use the plank at a height that will bring your head at eye level near the ceiling, thus avoiding stretching up to the work.

Papering or Painting Staircases

◄ For a straight flight of stairs, you will need a short ladder or adjustable three-way ladder or stepladder, a stepladder, and a plank.

◄ For a staircase that turns at a landing, you will need a short ladder or adjustable three-way ladder/stepladder (for the stairwell), a stepladder (for the top landing), a second stepladder or short ladder (for the middle landing), and two planks.

TIP! *Always pad the top of stepladders where they lean against the wall.*

Safety note: *Fix wooden lath to the landing floor for steps to rest against and tie planks together.*

Using Color

The choice of colors in a decorating scheme is, of course, a personal one; however, the particular colors used can be influenced by several factors.

Size of room The size and purpose of a room and its location may determine your choice of color. To make a small room appear larger and more spacious, the use of pale, receding colors such as pale blue, lavender, and cream can give the illusion of space, whereas the use of dominant, strong colors such as red, orange, and strong yellow will tend to make a large room seem smaller. Stronger colors are also useful for making surfaces appear nearer (such as high ceilings).

Purpose of room A living room can be made to feel cozy and welcoming by using warm colors such as reds, pinks, oranges, and yellows. A bedroom will have a restful atmosphere when pale and medium greens or blues are used.

Location of room A room that gets a lot of sunlight and tends to be warm can be given a cool color scheme by using pale to medium blues, lilacs, cool blue-greens, and greens. By contrast, a cold room that does not get much sunlight can be given a warming color scheme that uses pinks, reds, yellows, and oranges. A dark room can be improved with pale colors.

Color Terms

Without getting too technical, there are a number of terms used to describe and define color.

Hue Another name for the type of color—blue, green, yellow, red, and so on. For example, one might describe a color as having a bluish hue or a reddish hue.

Tone (or tonal value) This describes the lightness or darkness of a color, as when white or black is added to paint (this changes the tonal value).

Tint When white is added to a color, the resulting light color is often referred to as a tint.

Shade When black is added to a color, the resulting dark color is often referred to as a shade.

Chroma This term refers to the purity or intensity of a color; adding white or black to a color reduces its intensity.

Purity Refers to the strength of the color; purity is reduced when a color is mixed with another color or with white or black.

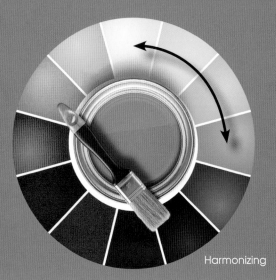

Harmonizing Colors

You might like to choose harmonizing colors, which are colors that are near or fairly close to each other on the color wheel: for instance, yellow, yellow-green, and green are harmonizing colors.

Harmonizing

Using Color in Schemes

An understanding of how colors are made will help you when choosing a color scheme. Colors are produced by mixing with other colors. For instance:

Red + yellow = orange

Yellow + blue = green

Blue + red = purple

Discordant colors These are sometimes used in a scheme to give emphasis or show off a feature, or provide a focal point. All colors have a natural order, from light to dark; for example, yellow is paler than blue and purple. If you use a particularly strong yellow with a light blue or lilac, thereby changing the natural color order, the results can look strange and give the impression of discord.

Matching colors Care has to be taken when using similar colors of the same tonal value (lighter or darker) together, as they do not always give a satisfactory effect and can appear to clash (or not work together). The old saying that a good contrast is better than a bad match can be true.

Color balance in schemes The proportion or amount of each color used in a scheme is important; if colors are used in the same amounts, the overall effect is less interesting than when you use varying amounts of color.

Note: Using darker colors in smaller amounts gives a well-balanced scheme.

Tonal values How light or dark a color appears can be influenced by the tone (lightness or darkness) of the adjacent color.

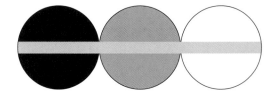

Contrasting Colors

You might prefer to choose contrasting colors, those that are opposite (or nearly opposite) each other on the color wheel. Yellow, for example, provides a contrast to blue and to purple.

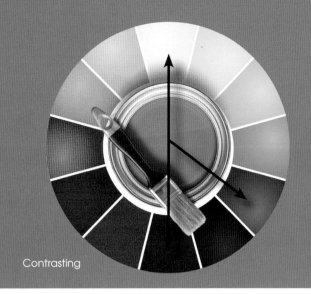

Contrasting

Here, the central identical gray strip is influenced by the different toned circles, appearing lighter against the black circle and darker against the gray and white circles. To prove that the center strip is exactly the same throughout its length, cover the upper and lower circles with pieces of white paper.

Hue How light or dark a color appears can also be affected by adjacent hues (colors). Try this experiment for yourself: take three sheets of colored paper in strong hues (say, bright yellow, strong blue, and vivid red). Also, find a sheet of mid-toned gray paper and cut it into three small identically sized rectangles. Place each small gray rectangle over the colored papers and note how the gray is influenced by each of the strong colors. Each identical gray rectangle will take on a different color cast. Notice also how the tonal value (lightness/darkness) of the inner rectangles is affected.

Hue is also affected by light, and colors can appear different when viewed in various light sources. Natural daylight (white light) gives the most accurate representation (A). Light bulbs (B) are a tungsten light source and give color a yellow tinge, while fluorescent lighting (C) can give color a greenish/bluish cast.

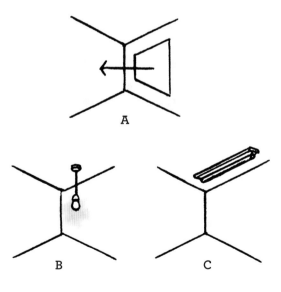

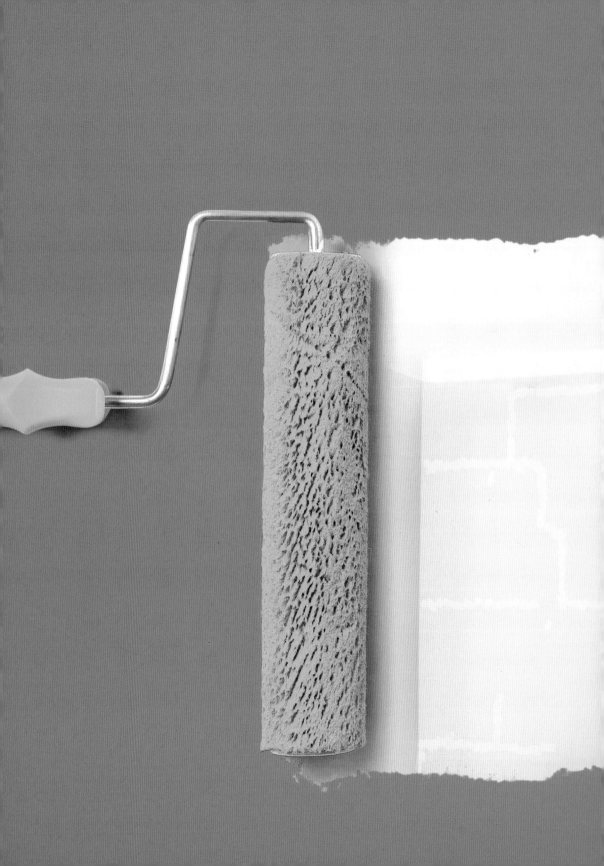

Part Two

Preparation

Surface Problems and Remedies

Flaking Painted Surfaces (Ceiling and Walls)

Description

Areas of a painted surface that have lifted and come away.

Possible Causes

- Lack of surface adhesion
- Lack of surface preparation: a powdery loose surface, which can be old whitening, or size-bound distemper, or paint which has become powdery with age
- Too many old coats of paint causing a heavy build-up on the surface
- Dampness on the surface
- Lack of adhesion between coats of paint

Remedy

Scrape off as much loose material as possible, wet, scrub and wash area. Sand down the edges of scraped area, apply filler to edges, and sand when dry (to help hide edges). Apply a coat of sealer (oil-bound is the most effective, see page 52). Allow sealer to dry thoroughly before applying finishing coats. Alternatively, use a steam stripper to soften loose coating, and scrape off as much as possible, then wet, scrub, and rinse the area. When dry, apply sealer coat.

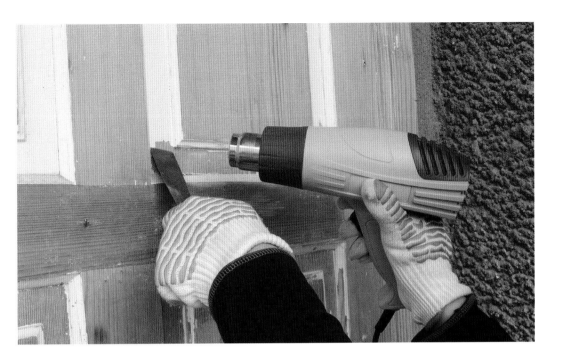

Flaking Textured Paint Surfaces (Ceilings and Walls)
Remedy

When this occurs, the only real remedy is to remove the texture coating.

Porous granular type finishes Remove by softening the paint with a steam stripper, and scraping off.

Nonporous texture coatings Strip it off using a special propriety texture paint remover (liquid or gel). Great care should be taken to protect the eyes and adequate ventilation to the room must be provided. It is a good idea to wear protective gloves. Always follow the product information. It is usually best to apply the remover to small sections of surface at one time.

DECORATOR'S DODGE
To protect the floor, cover the drop cloth with two layers of newspaper; this can then be rolled up with the mess inside at the end of the operation.

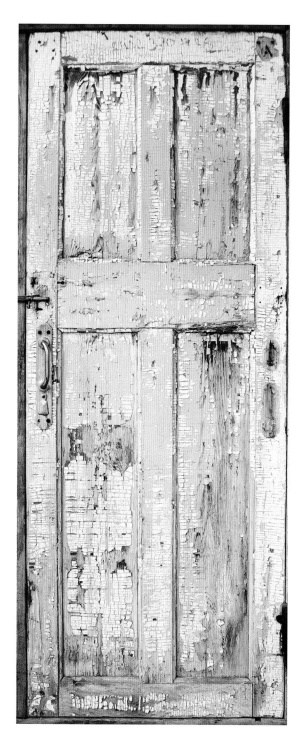

Cracking and Flaking Paint (Woodwork)

Description

Paint lifting and coming away from the surface.

Possible Causes

- Poor surface preparation: not sanding and undercoating before glossing = lack of key
- Not washing the surface, leaving it contaminated with dust and grease beneath the paint
- Aging of paint system: old coatings underneath losing adhesion, going powdery
- Action of weather, such as heat and frost
- Shrinkage of wooden surface
- Dampness

Remedy

Where possible, small affected areas can be scraped off, filled, sanded, and "spot"-primed. However, it is usually best to remove the paint by either burning off or by using a solvent paint remover (see page 45). Always make sure that paint remover is rinsed off thoroughly, and apply a good-quality primer before applying further coatings.

Wrinkled Paint Finish (Woodwork)

Description

Paint surface uneven with wrinkled uneven lines running across it.

Possible Causes

- Application of a fast-drying top coat, such as gloss over a soft coating
- Too much paint has been applied

Remedy

Make sure, before painting, that the previously coated surface is hard enough to take the new gloss. When applying paint, try not to apply too thick a coating.

Checking and Cracking (Fine Cracks) and Crocodiling (Deep Cracks)

Description

A series of interlacing cracks, usually all over the surface on painted woodwork.

Causes

- Differences of surface tension between coatings, resulting in movement of the adjacent coats, and shrinkage upon contraction of the top coat
- Application of fast-drying coatings over soft backgrounds, such as coatings that have not dried thoroughly
- In some cases, excessive heat can cause checking of paint

Remedy

It is often necessary to remove the affected paint coating by burning off or using solvent paint remover. Sometimes (but rarely) in the case of fine checking, the surface can be "flatted" (rubbed down) using wet-and-dry abrasive paper or soda block, and then well rinsed.

Rough, Gritty Surface

Description

Surfaces (usually painted surfaces) that contain gritty particles.

Causes

- Applying paint to surfaces that have not been rubbed down, or not dusted off after sanding
- Applying old paint that has dirt particles in it, such as bits of broken paint skin
- Using unclean brushes during application
- Surfaces that have aged and become granular or gritty, such as old plaster

Remedies

Always sand and dust off surfaces to be painted. Make sure that the paint has no bits of skin in it and is strained before use. A gritty paint surface can be flatted down with wet and dry abrasive or soda block paint remover.

Wherever possible, lightly sand, dust off, and apply an oil-based primer/sealer where surfaces such as old plaster have become gritty, to fasten down the surface. Unless the surface has become really gritty, granular, and very loose, then it is best to replace the surface by re-plastering, or by over-fixing a new surface such as plasterboard fixed to laths.

DECORATOR'S DODGE

Where there is a localized patch of powdery or granular plaster, it is sometimes possible to scrape, sand, and dust off, then apply a fine filler (mixed on the soft side). Then when dry, lightly sand, dust off, and apply a PVA sealer/adhesive diluted to a mix of 1 part PVA to 5 parts water. This should be allowed to dry thoroughly before decorating.

Note: Water-based paints should not be applied, unless the surface is first papered with lining paper (see Hanging Lining Paper, page 155).

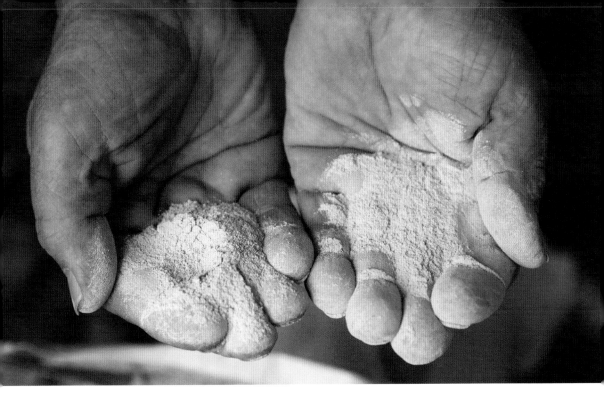

Chalk forms on the palm of the hand when it is placed on a powdery surface.

Powdery or Chalky Paint Surfaces

Description

A fine powder on the surface of paint.

Causes

- Applying paint to porous surfaces without first sealing the surface
- Ageing of the oily part of the paint
- Weathering of exterior paint

Remedies

Wash and scrub off loose powder as much as possible. It is then necessary to "fasten down" any remaining powdery paint with an oil-based sealer before applying further coatings.

Pattern Staining (Usually Ceilings)

Description

Dark areas striped with lighter-colored bands across them.

Cause

- Rising heat deposits dirt on ceiling surfaces. More heat passes between wooden laths and, therefore, leaves more dirt at those areas. The laths act as insulation.

Wooden laths in loft area form insulation.

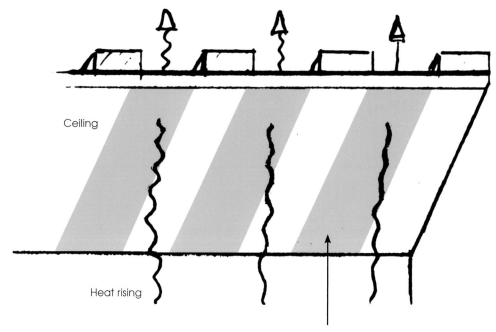

Ceiling

Heat rising

Greater deposits of dirt

Remedy

Scrub off and rinse as much dirt deposit as possible. When the surface is thoroughly dry, apply a stain-block primer. It is possible to get water-based primers, as it would be expensive to use stain-block aerosols over large ceiling areas.

Bleeding
Description

Certain substances come through paint coatings from behind. Water-based paints are more susceptible to bleeding than oil paint.

Possible Causes

- Red and purple dyestuffs, pen and felt pen markers, and red chalk
- Sooty areas
- Nicotine, tar, and creosote
- Rust spots caused by nails or bolts below the surface
- Resin from knots in wood and resinous wood
- Graffiti
- Damp stains usually show as large dark rings (on ceilings)
- Smoke marks (following a fire)

Circular damp stain on ceiling.

Remedies

Wherever possible, clean as much of the stain as is practical, using strong detergent, solvents such as methylated spirits and abrasives. When dry, seal with either "stain block" aerosol, stain block primer, or aluminum paint (which forms a barrier coating) or, in the case of resinous knots, apply shellac knotting overpainted with white undercoat.

Greasy Surfaces
Description

Surfaces that are obviously covered in a greasy deposit, or surfaces that, although not obviously greasy, will feel tacky to the touch.

Cause

- The gradual build-up of fatty cooking fumes, or fat splashes when frying food

Remedy

Remove the grease by thorough washing and scrubbing with detergent. If the grease build-up is heavy, it may be necessary to wash with a strong detergent or commercial wall cleaning solution, then rinse well.

Efflorescence
Description

White fluffy powder deposits on plaster (usually new plaster), bricks, and cement finishes, which can affect painted surfaces.

to go back into solution and later crystallize again as they dry out.

Following dry removal, keep checking the affected area over a period of time, and continue dry removal of any further salts. When they no longer appear, prime the area with an alkali-resisting primer before further decoration.

Saponification (Softening) of Oil Paint on Surfaces

Description

A strong active alkaline surface can in certain instances soften up and destroy oil-painted surfaces, turning the paint into soapy masses which often exude running areas of brown sticky liquid.

Cause

- Active alkaline salts, which are sometimes present in cement or in the mixing water used for the rendering of bricks

Remedy

Completely strip off the affected paint. Clean the surface. Make sure that the surface is dry before re-painting.

Note: Alkali-resisting primer is useful before painting.

Cause

- Alkaline salts, which are water-soluble, crystallize as white fluffy deposits when the water in a surface dries out

Remedy

Dust off the deposits or rub off with a dry rag, then wipe with a very slightly moist (not wet) cloth.

Note: Removal of the white deposits should not be done wet, as this will cause the salts

DECORATOR'S DODGE
After dry-wiping off the white salty deposits, lightly sand the affected area; this will "open up" the plaster surface, which allows any further accumulations of salt to dry out.

Black Mildew-Affected Surfaces

Description

A type of mold which forms on surfaces as small black patches or dots.

Causes

- Lack of ventilation
- Dampness
- Humidity (steam)

Remedies

Wash and scrub the affected area thoroughly with a strong detergent and disinfectant, followed by plenty of rinsing and drying off. If the condition persists, use a fungicidal wash and redecorate with fungicidal paint. It also helps to increase the amount of ventilation.

DECORATOR'S DODGE
Use a plastic scouring pad with detergent on persistent areas.

Wet Rot in Timber

Description

Sometimes called brown rot because of the dark brown color of the affected area.

Causes

- Dampness and prolonged soaking of the wood
- Also lack of ventilation in cold conditions

Remedy

Cut or chop out all affected wood and an area of good wood surrounding the rot. Then use a fungicide on any nearby masonry and replace with new wood.

Dry Rot in Timber
Description

The early stages of dry rot can be detected by "cubic cracking" along the grain of the wood and sometimes a musty pungent smell. In the later stages of dry rot there is a white furry body with silk-like strands.

Cause

- The germination of fine spores (like seeds); often forms where there is moisture, darkness, and warmth

Remedies

Destroy all affected timber and surrounding timber as soon as possible, and dispose of carefully.

Best advice: Call in experts immediately.

Raised or Proud Grain and Sunken Grain on Wood
Description

Where the grain of the wood stands up across the surface.

Causes

- Wood has not been smooth-plane finished
- OR wood has aged and weathered

Remedies

If the grain is highly raised Electric plane the surface and finish off with an electric sander.

If the grain is only slightly raised Surface-fill, applying filler that is on the soft side, using a filling knife at an angle slightly across the grain. When dry, lightly sand with a fine abrasive, again at an angle to the grain. When dry, apply primer coat.

DECORATOR'S DODGE
Add a small amount of white emulsion paint to a standard powder filler to make a fine grain filler.

Grain Texture or Fine "Ticks" in Wood
Description

Fine natural marks in wood grain. While these marks are generally acceptable under a wood finish such as stain or varnish, they do not enhance paint.

Remedy (for a paint finish)

- Use a fine grain filler across the grain

Tools for Preparation Work

Below is a selection of tools you might find useful when preparing your surfaces ready for decorating.

Sandpaper

Sanding block

Household plastic scouring pad

Drop cloths

Dust mask

Protective goggles

Scraper

Old flat brush for wetting in and scrubbing

Dust brush

Spackle knife

Wire brush

Glaziers knife

Shave hook

Blowtorch

Heat gun (electric)

Old leather gloves

Sponge

Rag

Rubber gloves

Two buckets

Washing Paint

DECORATOR'S DODGE
Rinsing off a ceiling can be done from the floor, using a long-handled sponge mop.

Dirt and residues such as nicotine or cooking grime should be washed off prior to decorating. Use a mild detergent or liquid soap in warm water.

1. Wet the surface from the bottom upward (to avoid streaks down the surface).
2. Scrub the surface from top downward using an old flat brush.
3. Rinse off with plenty of clean warm water and a fine-textured sponge.
4. Dry off with clean rags.
5. Allow the surface to dry thoroughly before applying paint.

For stubborn dirt (such as grease), use a soda block on surfaces to be painted.

1. Wet the surface.
2. Rub the surface with a soda block in a circular motion. **Note:** Do not dip the soda block in the water bucket as this can soften the block.
3. Rinse the surface off very thoroughly as traces of the caustic block, which are alkaline in nature, could be detrimental to paint coatings that follow.

DECORATOR'S DODGE
When washing gloss varnish, use water with a small amount of vinegar in it; this can get rid of "bloom" (misting) and restore the gloss.

Preparing Surfaces for Filling

1. Scrape off any loose surface areas.
2. Sand surface with sandpaper around a block of wood.
3. Rake out cracks with the side corner of a spackle knife.
4. Use the point of a shave hook to rake out large cracks.
5. Dust or brush off area.
6. Wet in large cracks with clean paintbrush.

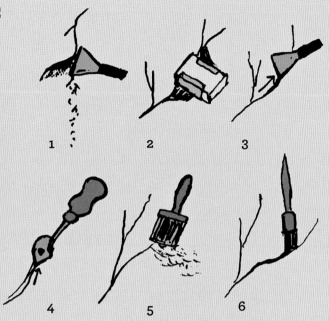

Mixing Filler

This should be done on a clean board by emptying an appropriate amount of filler (i.e. an amount that will be used before it hardens) to form a small pile (1).

Make a hollow impression in the middle of the pile; the back end of a scraper is good for this (2). Then add water to the hollow little by little (3) and gradually cover the water with filler, taken from the outside of the pile (4). Finally, mix the water and filler to a moist, but not sloppy, consistency. The correct consistency is important; if it is too wet, it will shrink, if it is too dry it will dry out too quickly and will be difficult to apply, and could crack.

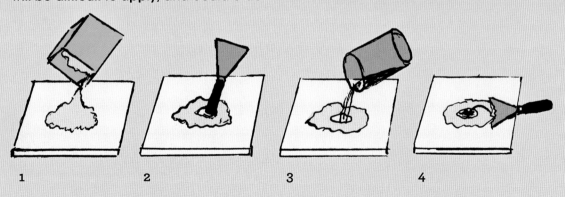

Filling Cracks and Irregularities

Sometimes it is necessary to fill cracks in surfaces you want to paint. You will need a variety of fillers depending on the surface you wish to fill (see below):

- Powder filler, interior
- Powder filler, exterior
- Powder filler, general-purpose
- Powder filler, fast-drying
- Ready-mixed filler in tubes and in tubs
- Wood filler, fine textured
- Chemically hardening wood filler; hardener in a tube or packet is added to the basic filler, mixed, and applied with a plastic spatula

Applying Filler to Surface Cracks

1. Scrape some filler off the mixing board. Filler should adhere to one side of the knife only.

2. Keep the back of the knife free of filler. Clean the knife by scraping it against the board.

3. Press the filler well into cracks.

4. Remove excess filler by dragging the knife along the filler. When completely dry, lightly sand the filler (only if necessary).

Notes: Deep cracks may need filling twice, because of shrinkage; it can be useful to first coat the area with PVA adhesive and allow it to dry before filling.

Some people prefer to leave the filling protruding slightly, then sand down when dry.

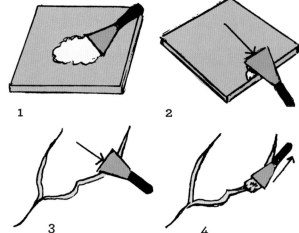

1

2

3

4

Applying Filler to Gaps Between Woodwork and Walls

1. If gaps are wide and deep, push rolled and moistened newspaper into the gap with the edge of a scraper before filling.

2. Press filler into the gap, keeping the knife at right angles to the gap.

3. Run a finger down the filler to lay off and drag off the surplus. **Safety note:** Watch out for sharp edges such as broken paint; a rubber glove can protect your hand.

4. Finally, lightly drag a moist sponge down the filled area. Do this very gently, so as not to wipe out the filler.

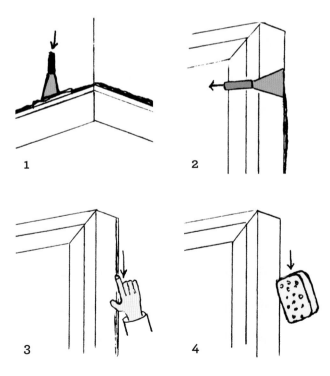

Applying Filler to Surface Imperfections

There is an old trade saying, "You can fill hollows, but you can't fill bumps." This is largely true, but you can minimize the effect of unavoidable bumps on surfaces as follows:

Chop Out Bump (If Possible)

1. If possible, chop out the bump using a bolster chisel and hammer.
2. Fill the hole made to build up the level (possibly more than once). It may be necessary to use plaster rather than filler.
3. Finally, once the filler is dry, block sand the area until level.

Sand Down Bump (If Possible)

This is a very dusty process, so wear a mask, goggles, and a hat. Use an orbital electric sander or an electric belt sander (preferably with a dust extraction system) to reduce the protruding bump.

Fill the Edges of the Bump

If the first two methods can't be applied, this method will reduce the effect of the bump.

1. Apply filler in such a way that it gradually tapers off into surrounding surface (chamfering).
2. The shaded area represents filling around the bump.

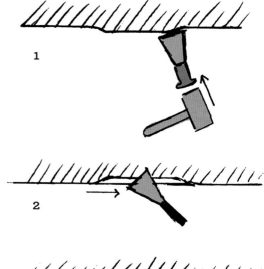

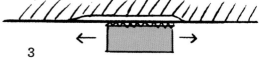

DECORATOR'S DODGE
A wide caulking tool is useful for laying off wide areas of filler.

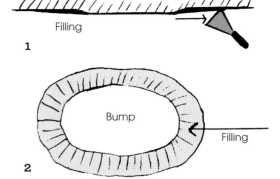

Filling

1

Bump

Filling

2

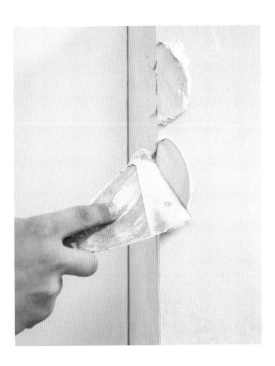

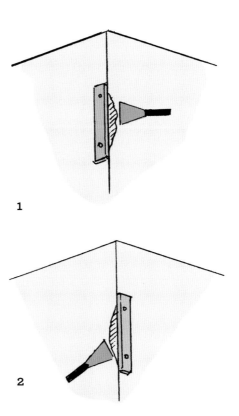

1

2

Repairing a Damaged External Corner

1. Hold or nail a flat piece of wood against the damaged corner, and apply filler or plaster against this.
2. When the filler is dry, place the wood at the other side of the corner (that has been repaired) and fill the second side.

Filling Holes
Stopping

This refers to filling holes in woodwork; filler such as putty or wood filler is applied to holes or joints. This is done with the point of a glaziers knife or plastic applicator strip. It is often necessary to apply more than one application, because of shrinkage.

Filling Large, Deep Areas

This may be necessary, for instance, where plaster has dropped off or is loose.

1. Knock off loose plaster areas. **Note:** If plaster sounds hollow when you tap it with the back of your fingers, then it probably is loose and requires removal.
2. Apply a PVA sealer/adhesive to exposed brickwork or background. Allow the PVA to dry, or at least to become tacky.
3. Mix up a one-coat plaster (white powder plaster/filler). If a large quantity of plaster is required for patching, it is easier to mix this in a bucket rather than on a flat board.
4. Apply with a wide scraper or pointing trowel or a plastering float.
5. Level off the plaster with a plastering float or wide spatula.
6. Allow the plaster to "set up" (harden off) and reapply a final leveling coat if needed and "float out."

Note: If there are small surface blemishes such as trowel line in the finish, it is possible to sand these down.

1

2

3

4

5

6

Tools Needed for Filling

Small brush
(for wetting in cracks)

Packet of filler

Tube of filler

Sponge

Plastic disposable gloves

Sanding block

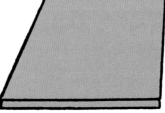

Large mixing board (or bucket lid)

Sandpaper

Scraper with a
flexible blade

Spackle knife and
shave hook
(used to rake out cracks)

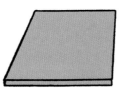
Small board to act as
a work off board

Bucket or container for water

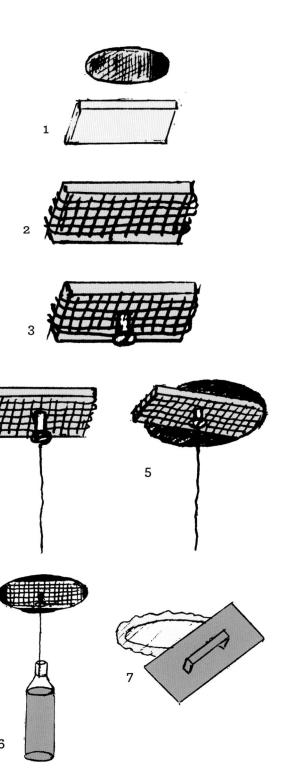

Filling a Hole in a Ceiling

1. Find a flat piece of wood slightly wider than the hole.

2. Attach mesh or fine wire netting to the face of the wood.

3. Fix a screw in the middle of the wood.

4. Tie a length of string to the screw.

5. Push the wood up into the hole, angling it to get it in.

6. Position the wood over the hole, tie a weight onto the string, or hold it down.

7. Apply one coat of quick-drying plaster/filler to face of wood and level off over hole.

8. Finally leave plaster to dry and harden before removing screw.

Using Abrasives

During the process of preparing surfaces for painting, it is often necessary to use abrasives in order to sand down rough edges. There are many types of abrasive on the market, each designed to use on a particular surface or in a specific situation. See the chart below for a breakdown of abrasives you might need when doing DIY decoration.

Tools to Use with Abrasives

In addition to sanding by hand, there are a number of electrical mechanical tools to help make the job easier.

Electric belt sander (A) Takes a continuous length of abrasive. Useful when large areas of surface need to be heavily sanded and smoothed off.

Disc sander (electric) (B) Uses various grades of sanding disc. Useful for general preparation of surfaces. Note: Tends to leave concentric sanding rings on the surface, if care is not taken.

Finishing sander (electric) (C) Uses small sheets of various grades of abrasive that fit onto an oscillating pad. Used for light sanding jobs.

Flap wheel (D) Small flaps or strips of abrasive held onto a central spindle. This fits into a "chuck" of an electric drill. Useful for sanding contoured areas.

Triangular (detail) sander (E) Uses special triangular-shaped sections of abrasive (fine grade to course). Handy for sanding small areas, particularly getting into the edges of surfaces, such as window sections.

Note: It is possible to get multi-purpose all-in-one sanders.

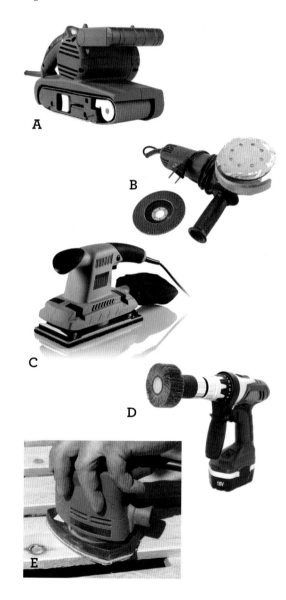

TYPES OF ABRASIVES	DESCRIPTION	USES
Sandpaper	Fine particles of sand held on pliable thick card backing. Supplied in sheets of fine to course grades.	General-purpose abrasive used when preparing surfaces, or for sanding down between coats of paint.
Aluminum oxide sandpaper	A very robust and hard-wearing material supplied in rolls or pieces cut from a roll.	General-purpose abrasive, as above.
Wet or dry sandpaper	A strong, flexible black sheet material that can be used as a dry abrasive or used with water.	Very useful for "flatting down" between coats of paint. Also useful where a surface needs to be cleaned as well as sanded.
Steel wool	Supplied in bundles, which vary in coarseness. Can be used dry or wet.	Useful when rubbing down intricate surfaces such as stair spindles. Can be used in conjunction with paint or varnish remover. Gloves are recommended.
Plastic scouring pads	Small pads of plastic fiber. Can be used wet or dry.	As above.
Wire brush	Wire filaments set into a wooden handle; vary in length and width.	Used mainly on metal surfaces for cleaning off rust. **Safety note:** Always wear protective goggles or safety glasses. Can also be used to "scuff" (remove the top surface of) washable wallpaper before stripping.
Liquid abrasive	A solution of abrasive particles, which is applied to painted surfaces, rubbed with a wet cloth, then rinsed off.	Useful for "flatting down" gloss paint.

Safety note: In addition to wearing a dust mask, eyes should be protected by safety glasses or goggles, especially when using electric sanders.

Sanding

Before Sanding

In addition to covering up carpets and furniture and masking off fittings, it is a good idea to keep the door of the room closed to prevent dust spreading to adjacent rooms. It is helpful to place a folded drop cloth at the bottom of the door and one spread out at the other side of the door. This will help to prevent dust and debris being trodden beyond the room.

Economy tip: Always tear full sheets of abrasive in half, then fold into three, giving you three fresh unused sides.

Wear a cap or hat, and be sure to wear a dust mask to avoid breathing in harmful particles. It is a good idea to open windows to increase ventilation.

Sanding Techniques

Large areas Sand in a series of circles, and wrap the abrasive around a block of wood.

Sanding Woodwork

New wood Always sand at a very slight angle across the grain.

Because new wood often has sharp corners and edges, sand these slightly to make them safer and less likely to split if they get hit.

Safety note: Wear a thick glove when sanding—it is easy to get splinters in your hands when sanding woodwork.

DECORATOR'S DODGE

Slap a used and clogged piece of abrasive hard onto a hard surface; this tends to unclog and prolong its use. Use worn sheets as a final sanding abrasive (except for delicate finishing).

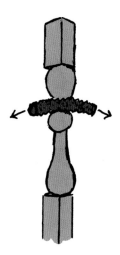

Intricate areas (such as stair spindles) Make a small roll of abrasive, which will make it easier to get into the contours.

Sand with the grain Always sand in the direction of the length of the woodwork, not across the length. Use a fine- to medium-grade abrasive, not coarse, which will tend to cut into the wood or the paint too much.

Sanding Between Coats of Paint

Sometimes called "de-nibbing," this is best done very lightly with a fine-grade abrasive to remove any small particles in the dry paint, without cutting into the surface. Some people prefer to use a fine grade wet-and-dry abrasive with water to "flat-down" between coats (thorough rinsing is very necessary with this method).

Sanding Down Surface Imperfections

To avoid stripping off paint in an area which has just a few imperfections such as old paint runs, it is possible to "take down" these areas using course abrasive and a sanding block, then finishing with a medium and fine abrasive. If there are a lot of imperfections, it is better to strip off the paint completely and start again.

After Sanding

It is essential to remove the surface dust, first with a dust brush, then with a clean, lint-free cloth dampened with mineral spirits. Or use a tack cloth.

Removing Defective Paint

There are three main methods of removing defective paint: using paint remover, using a hot air gun, or using a blowtorch.

Paint Remover Method

You can use two main types of solvent paint remover: one can be washed off and neutralized with water, while the second can be cleaned off and neutralized with mineral spirits.

Safety note: Regardless of which method you choose, wear rubber gloves and safety glasses, and provide plenty of ventilation.

1

1. Lay in only small amounts of surface at a time, using an old paintbrush to apply the paint remover.
2. Leave the remover to soak into the paint and form blisters.
3. Scrape off blistered paint.
4. Lay in stubborn areas of paint again and allow time for the stripper to work.
5. Scrape off the blistered paint.
6. Rinse surface well with either water or mineral spirits, depending on the type of stripper. A household plastic scouring pad is ideal for washing and rubbing down the surface.

2

3

Hot Air Gun Method (Electric)

This method is ideal for removing paint or varnish from woodwork. It is less likely to scorch the woodwork than a blowtorch, but is not as quick a method as the blowtorch method.

1. Remove the paint from moldings and intricate areas using a shave hook and the hot air gun before removing paint from the panels. The moldings take longer to strip and the paint remaining on the panels protects the wood.

2. Heat rises, so work from the bottom of the surface upward. This helps to prevent scorching of the upper areas.

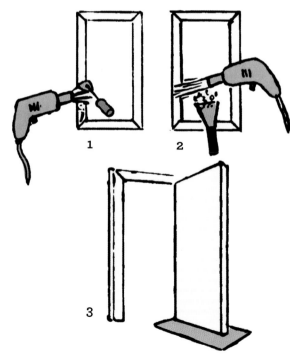

3. Place a piece of thin board such as hardboard beneath doors to protect the floor and catch the burning-off bits.

Blowtorch Method

This method employs mainly propane-type torches these days, and can be small canister types or a gas cylinder with a hose and a gun.

1. Do not point the gun directly at the glass. Move the gun rapidly up and down the surface, which pre-warms the glass.
2. Shield the glass with a wide scraper when burning off.

When Burning Off Paint

Keep the blowtorch well in front of the scraper or shave hook. If you are right-handed, use the scraper with the right hand and hold the blowtorch with the left hand; if left-handed, use the opposite hands.

Safety note: It is a good idea to wear a thick leather glove on the hand that holds the scraper. This means that if you accidentally get your hand in the way of the blowtorch flame, the glove will offer you some protection.

DECORATOR'S DODGE
Try to avoid burning off near glass. If this is not possible, before burning off, wave the torch or heat gun up and down the surface near the glass rapidly at right angles to the glass, in order to pre-warm the glass.

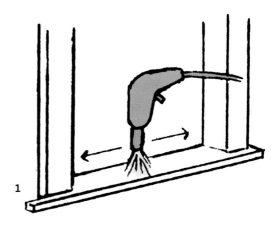

Part Three

Painting

Types of Paint

There are many different kinds of paint for different surfaces, uses, and finishes. Before we launch into how to paint, a brief outline of the types of paints available will help you decide which product is suitable for your particular decorating project.

Ultra matte

Description/ Uses	Water-based very flat finish, slightly grainy emulsion. Ideal for relatively new plaster surfaces, as it allows the plaster to "breathe" and dry out through it.
Advantages/ Disadvantages	Limited range of colors. Not easy to clean because of the flat paint finish. Easy to apply. Low odor.

Matte

Description/ Uses	Water-based finish for ceiling and walls, which can be wiped or gently washed.
Advantages/ Disadvantages	More resistant than ultra matte. Good range of colors, easy to apply. Low odor. Helps to hide surface imperfections.

Satin

Description/ Uses	Water-based finish for ceiling and walls with a sheen that can be wiped or washed easily. Useful in kitchens and bathrooms and higher "traffic" areas.
Advantages/ Disadvantages	Cleans easily. Good range of colors, easy to apply. Low odor. Tends to show any surface imperfections. Particularly effective for showing up textures or relief pattern surfaces.

Semi-gloss

Description/ Uses	Water-based finish for ceiling and walls. Can be cleaned, but to a lesser extent than satin.
Advantages/ Disadvantages	Same as satin.

Quick-drying eggshell finish, often containing a fungicide

Description/ Uses	Water-based finish for ceiling and walls. Some brands can be used on woodwork. Useful for steam resistance and surfaces that take reasonable wear and tear.
Advantages/ Disadvantages	Same as satin.

Eggshell finish (oil-based finish)

Description/ Uses	For ceilings, walls, and woodwork. Has a sheen. Suitable on surfaces that get a lot of wear and tear.
Advantages/ Disadvantages	Hard-wearing. Reasonable color range. Not as easy to apply as above and is difficult to clean out of brushes/rollers. Most have a high odor. Will show surface imperfections.

High gloss finish (oil-based)

Description/ Uses	Used mainly on woodwork, but sometimes used on ceiling and walls, where a resilient, hard-wearing finish is required.
Advantages/ Disadvantages	Very hard-wearing. Good range of colors. Easily washable. Good depth of gloss and "flows out" well. Requires some skill to apply. High odor. Requires oil undercoat. Equipment/brushes require cleaning out with mineral spirits.

Quick drying gloss (water-based)

Description/ Uses	Used mainly on woodwork, but sometimes on ceilings and walls.
Advantages/ Disadvantages	Easy to apply and quick drying. Good range of colors, wipeable. Low odor. Equipment can be washed out with water. Gloss not as high as oil; does not flow out as well.

Undercoat (oil-based)

Description/ Uses	Used on woodwork, ceilings, and walls, beneath oil-based gloss or eggshell finishes.
Advantages/ Disadvantages	Easy to apply. Covers previously painted surfaces easily. High odor. Requires mineral spirits as a thinner and brush cleaner.

Undercoat (water-based)

Description/ Uses	Used on woodwork, ceilings, and walls. Used mainly beneath water-based finishes.
Advantages/ Disadvantages	Easy to apply. Low odor. Previously painted surfaces need to be "flatted" well to provide a key.

"Non-drip" jelly paint

Description/ Uses	Sometimes referred to as "thixotropic" paints, these are usually gloss paints with oil base.
Advantages/ Disadvantages	Reasonable range of colors. Easy to apply. Brush marks tend not to flow out as easily as traditional oil gloss.

UPVC paint (water-based)

Description/ Uses	Used for painting ageing and graying plastic window frames and fascias.
Advantages/ Disadvantages	Quick-drying and easy to apply. Can contain a fungicide. Brushes can be cleaned with water. Short recoat time 4–6 hours.

Plaster sealer (water-based)

Description/ Uses	Intended for dry, porous, and powdery surfaces.
Advantages/ Disadvantages	Dries quickly; touch-dry 3–4 hours. Recoat time 6–8 hours. Low odor. Brushes can be cleaned with water. Needs to be thoroughly dry before recoating. Should not be used to cover stains.

Plaster sealer (oil-based)

Description/ Uses	Used on surfaces as above.
Advantages/ Disadvantages	Is suitable under an oil-based system. Slower drying than water-based and higher odor. Brushes have to be cleaned with mineral spirits.

Texturing paint (water-based)

Description/ Uses	Thick matte finish, sometimes self-colored (white). Used on ceiling and walls with texturing tools.
Advantages/ Disadvantages	Ideal for rough or uneven surfaces or to hide cracks. Cleans out with water. Various patterns can be applied. Not that easy to apply as only a workable amount can be laid in and textured at one time; porous surfaces first require a sealer coat (special water-based material). Finishes tend to have sharp edges and collect dust easily.

Masonry paint (oil- or water-based)

Description/ Uses	Smooth finish or granular. Used mainly on exterior work on most types of masonry as a decorative protective coating.
Advantages/ Disadvantages	Specially formulated to adhere to cement rendering and masonry. Offers good weather protection. Reasonable color range, low odor. The water-based varieties are vulnerable to the weather when still wet and can be affected by rain or frost. The oil-based type brushes are washed in mineral spirits.

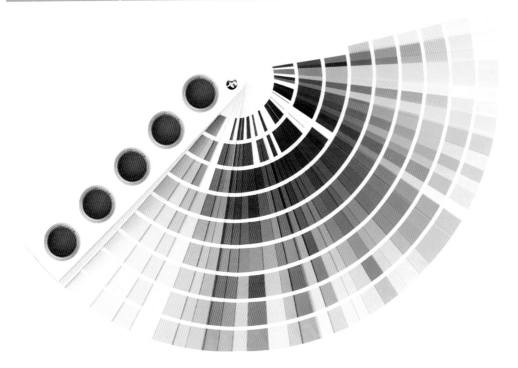

Special-Purpose Paints and Primers

Alkali-resistant primer
Based on tung oil.

Description/ Uses	Helps to prevent efflorescence (alkaline salts) from coming through a paint system.
Advantages/ Disadvantages	High odor. Slow drying. Only effective where the basic cause of salts (dampness) has been rectified.

Stain block primer
Usually water-based. Used mainly on ceilings and sometimes on walls.

Description/ Uses	Low odor. Relatively easy to apply. Effective against stains such as "pattern staining" (see page 23), providing that the surface is cleaned first.
Advantages/ Disadvantages	Has to dry out thoroughly before further coatings applied. May need more than one application.

Stain block primer (aerosol)
Synthetic solvent-based paint. Used as above.

Description/ Uses	Quick drying. More than one application can be applied quite quickly. Effective against stains as above.
Advantages/ Disadvantages	High odor. Inflammable. Nearby surfaces may require masking off against over-spray.

Damp-resisting paint
Usually based on chlorinated rubber.

Description/ Uses	Useful over areas that have been affected by dampness, providing that the basic cause of dampness has been remedied.
Advantages/ Disadvantages	Very high odor. Can be difficult to apply. Not easy to clean brushes/rollers, requiring special thinner. Low spreading rate.

Wood primer (oil)
Essential as first coat on new or old bare wood, underneath an oil-based system (undercoat and gloss).

Description/ Uses	Suitable for most woods. Relatively easy to apply. Forms a good bond to most types of wood.
Advantages/ Disadvantages	Slight odor. Brushes have to be cleaned out with mineral spirits or propriety brush cleaner.

Wood primer (water-based)
Used on most types of wood. Best used under a water-based paint system.

Description/ Uses	Low odor. Easy to apply. Brushes can be cleaned out in water.
Advantages/ Disadvantages	Not suitable for some oily or resinous woods. May not penetrate the wood to the same degree as oil-based product.

Fire-retardant paint
Usually synthetic base, often referred to as "intumescing" coatings, designed to bubble up and form a protective layer when on fire.

Description/ Uses	Effectively forms a "blanket" coat against fire. Cuts down the "flame spread" and combustibility rate of surfaces.
Advantages/ Disadvantages	Can be expensive. Relatively high odor. Limited color range.

Floor and ceramic tile paint
Synthetic finish, formulated to adhere well to stone, concrete, and ceramic tiles.

Description/ Uses	Covers well. Dries fairly quickly.
Advantages/ Disadvantages	High odor. Limited color range. Usually requires special thinner.

Fungicidal paint

May be oil- or water-based. Used on problem areas where black mildew has been present.

Description/ Uses	Water-based dries quite quickly and is easy to apply.
Advantages/ Disadvantages	Oil-based has a higher odor than water-based. Surface requires cleaning first, and ideally a fungicidal wash applied. Recommend protective gloves.

Blackboard paint (oil-based)

An absolute matte black finish intended for chalk boards.

Description/ Uses	Quick-drying, covers well.
Advantages/ Disadvantages	Some odor. Requires mineral spirits to clean out brushes.

Heat-resisting paint (synthetic base)

Intended as a finish, usually gloss. Used on surfaces that get very hot.

Description/ Uses	Does not discolor easily. Tends to be quite thick to apply and may require heat to help it dry.
Advantages/ Disadvantages	Limited color range. Some odor. May require special thinners to clean out brushes.

Cellulose finish (cellulose-based)

Intended as a hard-wearing finish on metal (usually gloss). Used mainly on cars, applied by spray gun or as aerosols.

Description/ Uses	Very hard-wearing. Reasonable color range.
Advantages/ Disadvantages	High odor. Not usually brushable. Requires skill to apply. Needs cellulose thinners. Usually spray gun is needed.

Lacquers (synthetic base)
Intended as hard-wearing finishes on wood or metal.

Description/ Uses	Very hard-wearing.
Advantages/ Disadvantages	High odor. Not easy to apply. Limited color range.

Aluminum wood primer (oil-based)
Contains aluminum pigment in granular form. For use on many types of wood.

Description/ Uses	Adheres well to wood and forms a "barrier coating" over certain oily or resinous woods.
Advantages/ Disadvantages	High odor. Not too easy to "cover" with subsequent coats of white undercoat.

Metallic paint finishes (oil- or lacquer-based)

Description/ Uses	Many metallic finishes have a pigment with "leafing" quality, which gives good obliterating power and shiny finish.
Advantages/ Disadvantages	High odor. Requires special thinners.

DECORATOR'S DODGE
Aluminum finishing paint can sometimes be used to obliterate stains on surfaces. Due to the "leafing" quality of the paint, it forms a barrier.

Metal Primers

These products are designed to adhere well to ferrous metals, such as iron and steel, or non-ferrous metals, such as aluminum, copper, and brass.

General all-purpose metal primer (oil-based)
Can be applied to most ferrous and non-ferrous metals.

Description/ Uses	Very versatile; for use on iron and steel, aluminum, copper, etc.
Advantages/ Disadvantages	Can require a long drying time. Needs to be completely dry before further coatings can be applied. Really intended under oil-based paints.

Quick-drying acrylic metal primer (water-based)
For use on new bright or weathered galvanized metal.

Description/ Uses	Quick drying 2–4 hours, recoatable after 6 hours. Low odor. Brushes can be cleaned out with water.
Advantages/ Disadvantages	Not recommended on heated surfaces or where there is high humidity and condensation.

Red lead primer (oil-based)
For use on iron and steel.

Description/ Uses	Gives good protection.
Advantages/ Disadvantages	Slow-drying. Dark color may be difficult to obliterate. Brush marks may not flow out easily.

Metal primer, red lead (water-based)

Description/ Uses	Quicker drying than traditional red lead. Easy to brush on and flows out evenly.
Advantages/ Disadvantages	Not suitable on heated metal surfaces and non-ferrous metals.

Chromate metal primer (synthetic base)
Used on ferrous and non-ferrous metals.

Description/ Uses	Versatile primer, as it can be used on iron and steel or aluminum and aluminum alloys. It is easier to cover than red lead, as it is lighter colored (gray-green). Can be used on heated surfaces.
Advantages/ Disadvantages	Slow-drying. Some odor. Brushes need thinners or mineral spirits.

Calcium plumbate metal primer (synthetic base contains lead)
For application to new, untreated galvanized iron/steel.

Description/ Uses	Eliminates the need for pre-etching treatment. Light colored, cream. Can be used on wood as well as metal; useful where both metal and wood exist together, such as some types of window frames.
Advantages/ Disadvantages	Slow-drying. Some odor. Brushes need thinners or mineral spirits.

Twin-pack etching primer (synthetic base)
For use on untreated aluminum and intended as a pre-treatment under a suitable primer (not as a primer in itself).

Description/ Uses	Ensuring good adhesion of subsequent primers and following coatings. Light colored (pale yellow).
Advantages/ Disadvantages	Needs to be fully dry, at least 12–16 hours before recoating. Some odor. Two parts need to be mixed together and has limited "pot life" once mixed. Requires special thinners.

Single-pack etching primer (synthetic base)
For sealing zinc and aluminum metal-sprayed steel. Used mainly on site as a metal treatment prior to priming.

Description/Uses	Simple way of sealing on-site sprayed metal surfaces.
Advantages/Disadvantages	Highly inflammable, low flash point. Needs to be fully dry as above. Needs special thinners. Still requires priming. Not intended for normal household use.

Micaceous iron oxide (oil-based)
High-build thick coating for use primarily on steelwork.

Description/Uses	Offers long-lasting protection against corrosion. Can be used as a finishing coat in some cases.
Advantages/Disadvantages	Slightly colored, textured finish; is more suitable for heavy steel structures. Slow-drying. Mineral spirits needed for brush cleaning. Has an odor.

Bituminous paints
Protective coating often used on iron and steel.

Description/Uses	Resistant to moisture. Very protective, flexible coat.
Advantages/Disadvantages	Some odor. Can cause "bleeding" to subsequent paint coatings. Limited color range, such as dull reds and browns, aluminum, dark gray, and black. Brushes need special thinners.

Bituminous coatings (black)

Description/Uses	General-purpose weatherproof finish for surfaces such as metal, concrete, etc. Ideal for surfaces in contact with drinking water.
Advantages/Disadvantages	Some odor. Slow-drying. Brushes require thinners. If applied over existing paint, it can soften it. Bleeding (staining) can occur. Limited color range (dull reds and browns).

Wood Stains, Preservatives, and Varnishes

There is a confusing number of products (both oil- and water-based) designed to enhance and protect wood, but broadly speaking they can be split into three categories: those for exterior use, those for interior use, and those that can be used both on exteriors and interiors.

Wood Stain

Wood stain can be either semi-transparent (which allows the natural grain of the wood to show through) or opaque (which offers a colored alternative, and is often used where the natural color of the wood is to be changed). Wood stains can also be sub-divided into high-build and low-build finishes.

High-build wood stains are thicker (more viscous) than low-build wood stains, and protect the wood by a creating a thick film coating. They work by partially penetrating the wood and by clinging to the wooden surface.

Low-build wood stains are thinner, and to be effective, rely on penetrating the wood as well as forming a thin coating on the surface.

Preservatives

Sometimes referred to as preservative basecoat, these products are intended to penetrate deeply into untreated wood and protect it against rot and ultraviolet rays. These preservatives are sometimes a treatment in themselves, or are often applied before the wood stain, but in many cases (just to confuse things further), there are products described as preservative wood stains that both preserve and give a stained finish.

Coatings That Simulate Wood Stain

These products are used where a wood effect is required on top of a previously painted surface, or where an uneven wood finish needs obliterating. They consist of a colored base coat, which, when dry, has a semi-transparent top coat that is applied sparingly and then brushed out rather coarsely to simulate wood grain (rather like the old-fashioned graining scumble). The product needs at least 16 hours to dry between coats and sanding should be avoided. The top coat dries to a sheen finish.

What to Choose?

So from all this confusion, how do you decide which product to use? In order to come to some decision, the following factors need to be considered:

- Is the product to be used on exterior or interior woodwork?
- What degree of wear and tear will the finished surface be exposed to?
- Is the product just to enhance and decorate, or does it need to preserve and protect the wood, or does it need to do both?
- Do you want to hide or change the color of the existing wood surface?
- Do you want a matte finish or one with a sheen?
- Does a strong odor matter? For instance, are you using it in a kitchen or a bedroom where it may matter? If so, choose a water-based stain that has less odor than an oil-based product.

If in doubt, consult the various product information leaflets, which are often available in the store where you buy the products. You may also read the information usually displayed on the side of the product's container.

Wood Dyes

These are thin spirit-based liquid colors that usually come in wood colors such as teak, mahogany, oak, etc. These penetrate bare wood surfaces to change the original color. The dye-coated wood usually needs overcoating with a finish such as varnish.

Varnishes (Oil- or Water-Based)

There are two categories of varnish: interior and exterior quality, which come in either gloss, eggshell, satin sheen, or matte.

Natural Wood Finishes

Products such as teak oil (for teak wood) and boiled linseed oil (for oak) enhance the natural color of woods, but tend to be slow-drying and not as protective as high-build varnish.

Measuring for Paint

Before estimating the quantity of paint you will need, remember that how far a can of paint will go is affected by the following factors:

- Porosity (amount of suction) of the surface
- Whether the surface is smooth or rough or textured
- Type of paint
- Viscosity (thickness) of the coating.

Measuring Ceilings

Note that the easiest way to measure a ceiling is to measure the floor beneath it (if possible). Measure the length times the width to get the square area.

Measuring Walls

To measure a single wall or part of a room, measure the height of the wall and multiply by the length of the wall to get the square area.

To measure all the walls of a room, measure the walls' heights and multiply by the perimeter of the room (length around the room) to get the square area.

Measuring Woodwork

Smaller areas such as doors and windows can be measured individually, then the areas added together to give a total square area.

Width

Length

Calculating

When you have measured up and obtained the square area, you can use the manufacturer's suggested coverage figures on the paint can (or paint leaflet) to work out how much paint is needed. For example:

You measure the perimeter of a room and the height and multiply the two to arrive at the square area, say 76 square yards (approximately 64 m²). The manufacturer's suggested spreading rate is 19 square yards (16 m²). Then if you divide the 76 square yards by the 19 square yards, you will find that you need 4 quarts of paint.

Note: Remember, paint goes further when second-coating (having reduced the suction), so you can calculate less paint for the second coat.

Typical Areas Covered by Paint per Quart

Vinyl silk: 17–19 square yards (14–16 m²)

Vinyl matte emulsion: 16–20 square yards (13–17 m²)

Undercoat: 19 square yards (16 m²)

Gloss: 20 square yards (17 m²)

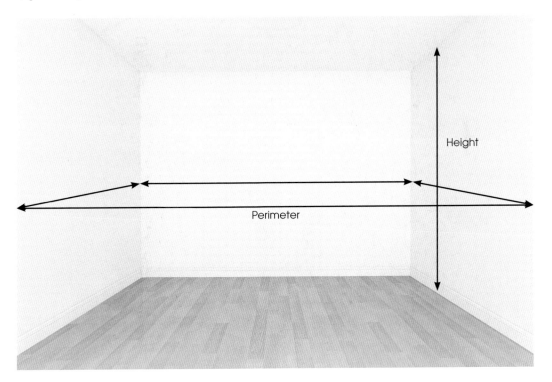

Height

Perimeter

Tools for Painting

Equipment for painting comes in a baffling array—brushes, rollers, protective materials, and trays are among the necessary items you may need to acquire before you start to work on your project.

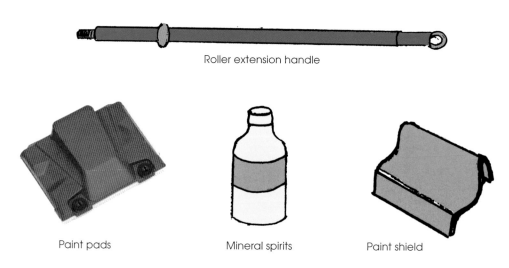

Roller extension handle

Paint pads

Mineral spirits

Paint shield

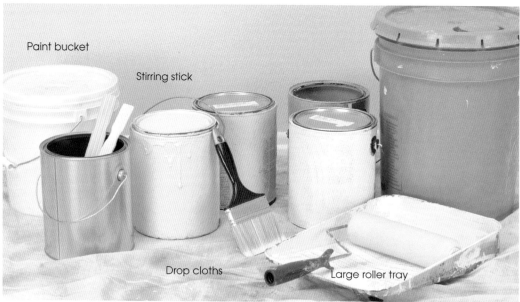

Paint bucket

Stirring stick

Drop cloths

Large roller tray

Masking tape

Small foam rubber
roller and tray

Rag

Brushes
7 in. (178 mm) flat brush
2¾ in. (68 mm) or
3 in. (76 mm) paintbrush
1½ in. (38 mm) paintbrush
½ in. (13 mm) paintbrush
Fitch

Stirring stick

Large or medium pile roller

Getting Ready to Paint

Before you begin to paint, it is important that you protect the furniture and fittings in the room in which you plan to decorate. While it might be preferable to move furniture out of a room, sometimes this is not possible.

1. Move large furniture items away from the walls to the center of the room.
2. Leave gaps between some items of furniture; this will allow you to move from one side of the room to the other when painting ceilings using a roller on an extension pole handle.
3. Move smaller pieces of furniture around the larger ones and remove ornaments and pictures to another room. Chairs can be stacked upside down on top of each other or on top of settees or sofas.
4. Cover up furniture with drop cloths or plastic sheets.
5. Cover up the floor area with drop cloths; old bed sheets will do, but it's best to use double them, as they are not as thick as drop cloths. Newspapers are handy for smaller areas.
6. Protect light fittings, including wall lights, by draping or wrapping sheets of newspaper around them and fastening them in position with masking tape. You may also slip plastic bags over the fittings.

Safety note: It is important that the light bulbs are removed to avoid any fire risk.

Preparing Paint for Use

Before opening a can of paint, dust off the lid and the can's grooves. Always place a hand over the top of the paint can lid when levering it off; this will prevent the lid flying up and scattering paint upward.

The best and safest way to lever off a paint can lid is to place the screwdriver or flat-bladed knife sideways into the edge of the lid groove, and *not* at right angles to the lid where it can slip.

Removing Paint Skins

1. If the top of the paint has formed a skin, cut around the edge of the skin where it meets the edge of the can with the point of a putty knife, chisel knife, or a wide screwdriver.

2. Next grip hold of the middle of the skin and lift it out (disposable gloves are useful for this).

3. Place this in an old empty can or on a double sheet of newspaper. The skin can be folded up inside and disposed of.

1

2

3

DECORATOR'S DODGE

Sometimes a paint skin will not form very thickly and is too flimsy to get hold of easily. So after cutting around the edge of the skin, place a small square of newspaper onto the center of the skin. Grip hold of this and remove the skin, which will be stuck to the paper.

Stirring Paint

Using a clean, flat, narrow stir stick, stir in a circular motion, first clockwise, then counter-clockwise.

Lift the stick up and down as you continue the circular stirring; this helps to mix the pigment into the paint media.

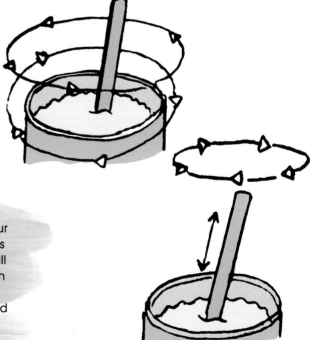

DECORATOR'S DODGE

When using more than one can of a particular color, it is a good idea to pour the cans into a large container (such as a bucket) and stir them together. This will avoid any slight color changes that can occur between one and another. If the bucket has a lid, the paint can be stored in this.

Straining Paint

Sometimes paint becomes contaminated with bits, either pieces of broken paint skin or dirt introduced from the surfaces being painted. It is therefore necessary to remove these by straining the paint. This can be done by passing the paint through an old kitchen sifter, or by passing it through a piece of pantyhose, which can be attached to a paint bucket with either an elastic band or string.

The Advantages of Using a Paint Bucket

Using a paint bucket has several advantages:

- A paint bucket holds a smaller quantity than the stock can and is, therefore, lighter and more convenient to hold and carry.
- The paint left in the stock can remains untouched and, therefore, stays clean.
- If the lid is replaced onto the stock can, the paint is not exposed to the air and, so consequently, does not thicken up.
- A paint bucket is not as deep as the stock can, so it is easier to dip brushes into it.

DECORATOR'S DODGE

Attach string or wire across the paint bucket from the two handle fixings. This makes it possible to scrape off excess paint and lay the brush conveniently across the wire.

DECORATOR'S DODGE

A good method of keeping a paint bucket clean is to use a plastic container inside the bucket (for the paint). A good makeshift plastic container can be made easily by cutting an empty soda bottle in half. A 3-liter (6-pint) bottle is a good size, although a 2-liter (4-pint) bottle will do. An added advantage is the area between the plastic container and the paint bucket, where it is possible to stand paintbrushes during use.

How to Use a Paintbrush (Undercoating and Glossing)

Safety note: Always keep the room well ventilated.

When Using a New Paintbrush for the First Time

1. Before dipping into the paint, bend the bristles backward and forward to get rid of any loose hairs.
2. Dip the bristles into the paint, no more than two-thirds of the way up the bristle.
3. Dip the loaded brush against the inside of the paint bucket to get rid of surplus.

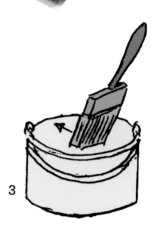

1

2

3

DECORATOR'S DODGE

- Before applying gloss paint, warm the room. Gloss flows better and "checks" (reaches its initial drying stage) more easily.

- To help prevent paint runs or sags, point a fan heater at the door (not too close, though) following glossing. First make sure that the floor is clean.

- To check that paint is dry, always use the back of your fingers, not the tips, which can leave marks.

How Do I Know How Much Gloss to Apply?

1. As you brush the gloss onto the surface, it should flow easily without too much "pull" on the bristles.

2. When you "lay off" the gloss, there should be a certain amount of pull on the bristles.

Do not overbrush, as this can cause the paint film to roll back on itself and not cover very well.

Do not underbrush, since this can cause paint build-up and "sags," "runs," and "curtains" (see page 114).

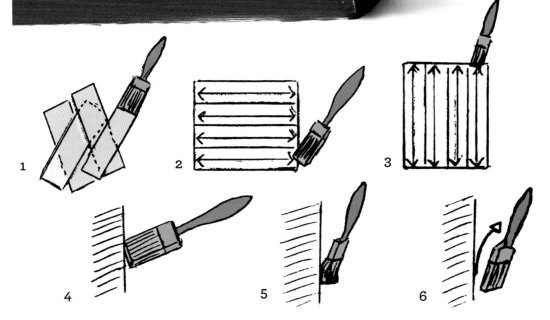

Applying the Paint

1. Apply the paint in random overlapping strokes.

2. Lay out the paint with horizontal cross strokes.

3. Lay off vertically, finishing on upstrokes.

4. If applying undercoat, use the tips of the bristles during the final lay off.

5. If using gloss paint, use the sides of the bristles during the final lay off.

6. Lift the brush off the surface as you come to the end of the laying-off stroke.

Painting Woodwork

Always try to keep a "wet edge" when painting (that is, try to keep moving the outer edge of where you are painting). This avoids overlapping brush marks and runs. To do this it is best to work to an application sequence (see below):

Painting Flush Doors

1. Remove door furniture, handles, finger plates, etc.
2. Paint the door edges first.
3. Work in small rectangles (see numbered diagram, below).
4. Blend each painted block into the next with both horizontal and vertical brush strokes.

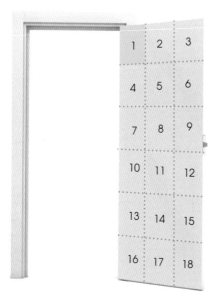

Note: Brush the paint outward toward the edges (see above). This avoids paint build-up and possible runs at the edges.

1

2

How to Paint Each Side of a Door a Different Color

1. Paint the hinged edge of the door the same color as the closing face of the door.
2. Paint the outer edge of the door the same color as the side that faces the room.

DECORATOR'S DODGE
Always brush paint in the direction of wood grain; if there is no grain, then brush with the length of the item.

Painting Paneled Doors

1. First paint the edge of the door.
2. Next paint the moldings, then the panels. Repeat on the other panels.
3. Paint the vertical center rails.
4. Paint the horizontal cross rails.
5. Paint the two outer vertical styles.
6. Paint the doorframe. Cut in the edges before the faces of the frame.

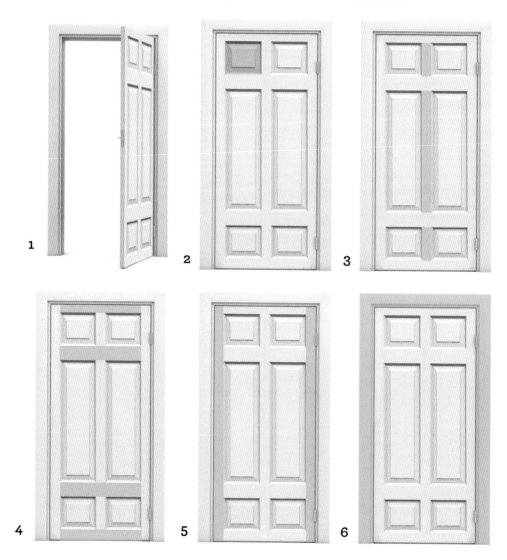

Laying Off Panels

1. Press the tips of the bristles just below the top moldings and lay off downwards, lifting the brush off at the end of each stroke.

2. Press the tips of the bristles above the bottom moldings and lay off upwards with the side of the bristles. Lift the brush off at the end of each stroke.

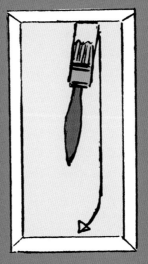

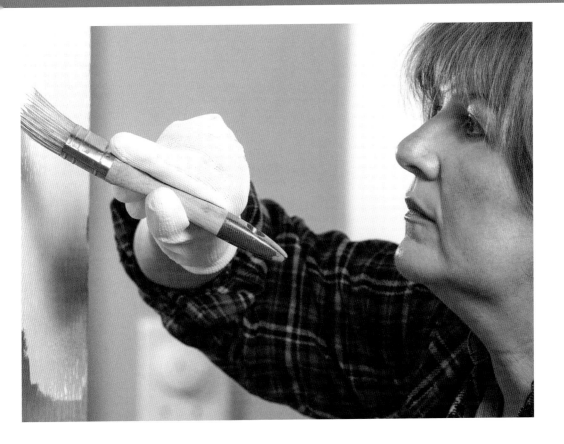

Painting a Small-Paned Casement Window with Glazing Bars (Muntins)

Paint the hinged window edge of opening casements before actually tackling the window itself.

1. Paint the inner glazing bars.
2. Next, paint the upper and lower glazing bars.
3. Paint the vertical glazing bars.
4. Next, paint the two side members (thick members).
5. Paint the upper and lower thick members.
6. Lastly, paint the windowsill, and if the window has wooden side reveals, paint these as well.

1

2

3

4

5

6

Painting a Sliding Sash Window

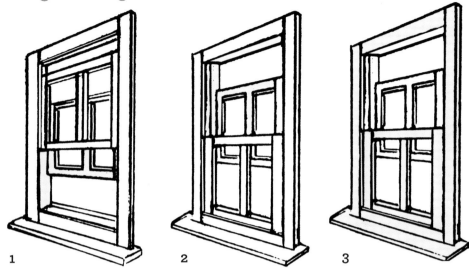

1
2
3

1. Cross over the upper and lower sashes, i.e. move the bottom sash up and the top sash down. Then paint the bottom section of the top sash, and the bottom edge of the bottom sash. Next, paint all the exposed runner sides.
2. Cross over the sashes (top sash toward the top and bottom sash back to the bottom). Paint the remainder of the top sash and the exposed top runner tracks.
3. Finally, paint the lower sash, including the top edge, and paint the surrounding moldings, the tracks, and the windowsill.

Note: Leave both sashes slightly open while the paint dries. It is a good idea to move the sashes up and down a few times, as soon as the paint is dry enough to handle. This keeps them from sticking.

Painting Louvres (Door or Window Shutters)

Because of the difficulty of getting between the louvre blades with a brush, it is best to use a small painting pad between the laths, and finish off the front edges with a brush.

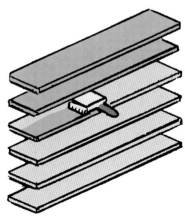

Cleaning a Paintbrush (Oil Paint)

Brushes in oil paint can be kept soft for short periods, such as overnight, by standing the bristles in a pot of water. Do not allow the water to cover the metal stocks, as water can cause rusting, get into the stocks and cause problems when painting.

Cleaning a Brush

1. Scrape out as much paint from the brush as possible by scraping it on the rim of the can.

2. Wash the brush out several times with mineral spirits in a paint bucket or empty can. Place dirty mineral spirits in an old can or screw-top jar.

3. Wash brushes in hot water with liquid soap. Repeat steps 2 and 3 until clean.

DECORATOR'S DODGE

- When used mineral spirits have been kept in a sealed container, the paint sediment will settle to the bottom, and it is possible to pour the mineral spirits off carefully (or strain it), and use it again for further brush cleaning.

- After washing a brush in mineral spirits, the mineral spirits can be removed by twirling the brush rapidly between the palms of the hands into an empty can or bucket.

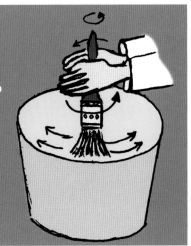

Staining and Varnishing Woodwork

Varnishing is very similar to glossing; however, wood stain requires a few extra skills.

Safety note: Always keep the room well ventilated, with windows open, if possible.

1. As with paint, always stain or varnish the edges first, and wipe off any stain on the faces.
2. Apply wood stain and varnish in the direction of the wood grain, usually with the length of the object being stained.
3. Try to work a small area at a time and avoid overlapping onto other sections; if you do overlap, dab off with a rag.
4. Keep a "wet edge" moving along the grain, especially with wood stains.
5. Sometimes it is easier to apply wood stain with a piece of rag instead of a brush.
6. Never "leave off" a section of work partway through, and try to complete all of one section at one time.
7. If you have to stain a large area, work in narrow strips along the grain and keep a "wet edge" moving.
8. When using wood stain, avoid working in sections as overlaps can show.

1

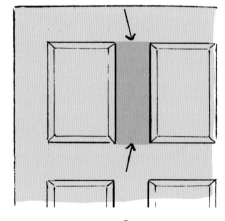

2

3

4

5

6

7

8

Glossing with a Disposable Sleeve Roller (Foam Rubber Sleeve)

In order to prevent your hands from getting splattered with gloss paint, you might consider wearing either disposable or rubber gloves.

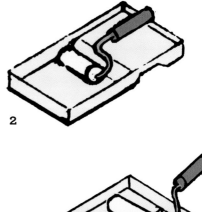

1

2

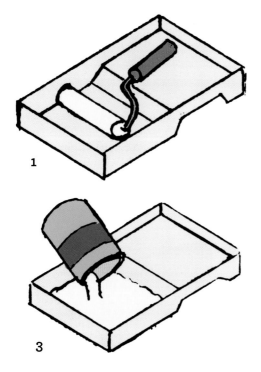

3

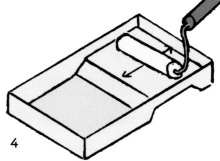

4

1. Gloss can be applied to wide areas with a 7-in. (175-mm) wide roller, using an appropriately sized roller tray.
2. Gloss can also be applied to smaller areas with a 4 ½-in. (114-mm) wide roller, using a smaller roller tray.
3. Partially fill the deep end of the tray with paint.
4. Dip the roller into the paint and work out the roller on the shallow end of the tray to get the paint to spread evenly onto the sleeve.
5. Roll the paint onto the surface in random diagonal bands.
6. Lay off in vertical bands using the roller very lightly.
7. If preferred, lay off lightly with the tips of a brush after roller lay off; this gets rid of the slight "orange peel" texture left by a roller.

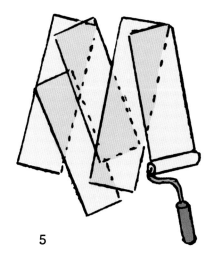

5

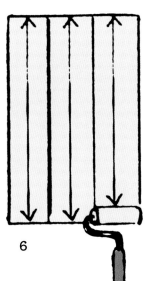

6

7

Types of Roller

Paint rollers come in various widths and diameters—two common widths are 9 in. (229 mm) and 7 in. (178 mm). Roller sleeves are either:

- Short pile for applying oil eggshell and gloss
- Medium pile for applying water-based paint on flat surfaces
- Long pile for applying water-based paint over textured surfaces or over relief patterns.

When choosing a paint roller, a "birdcage" wire frame type is useful, because you can slide the sleeve on or off easily when washing out or when changing color (using two sleeves).

Note: During the time when the paint is being applied, the paint roller makes a slight sound as it spreads out the gloss. As the paint is being spread out the sound is reduced, which means that the paint is ready for lay off. There should be hardly any surface noise during final roller lay off.

Storing a Foam Rubber Roller Sleeve

Foam rubber roller sleeves are regarded as disposable after use. However, it is possible to prolong the life of a sleeve for short periods such as overnight.

1. First, scrape as much paint as possible back into the tin using the side of a scraper or putty knife.

2. Wrap the roller sleeve with a damp rag.

3. Place the sleeve (with damp rag) inside a plastic bag.

4. Use a bag twist fastener to close the bag.

5. Place the bag containing the roller into an empty bucket and store in a cool place, such as a cellar.

6. The next day, "work out" the roller on a clean piece of board or card to get rid of any moisture. **Note:** Ink from newspaper tends to come off onto the roller.

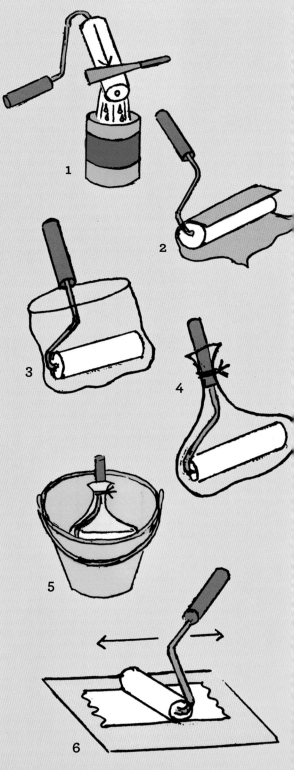

Using a Roller to Paint Ceilings

The easiest and most convenient method for painting ceilings is to use a roller extension pole handle. This means that you only have to resort to using steps when brushing the edges and corners of the ceiling.

1. Try to work in narrow strips of about 18 in. (458 mm) or two roller-widths, and keep a "wet edge" (a wet outer edge). **Note:** An average room with a width of about 10 ft. (3 m) will need about four roller dips to do a strip across the ceiling 18 in. (458 mm) wide.

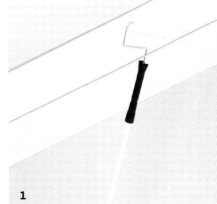

2. Do not roll the paint out too far as this can cause "roller skip." Always work from the light source (usually the window) so that it is possible to see by the shine of the paint whether the ceiling is all coated.

Tip: To avoid getting sprayed with "roller drizzle," roll slowly with a fully loaded roller, then it is possible to lay off more quickly. It is a good idea to wear gloves, a cap, and a long-sleeved shirt.

Using a Roller to Paint Walls

Work from right to left if right-handed and from left to right if left-handed.

1. Work in narrow bands (top to bottom of the wall) and keep wet outer edges, work from the light source, usually a window.
2. When painting one small wall, such as a fireplace wall, work in horizontal strips from the top to the bottom of the wall.

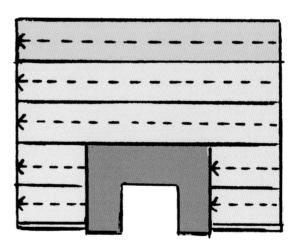

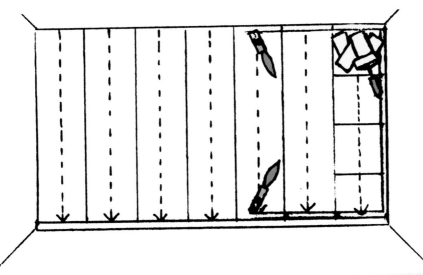

Note: When rolling paint onto textured or embossed patterned surfaces, the paint will not spread as far as on a smooth flat surface. On a flat surface, which has been painted before, one roller dip will cover an area approximately 30 x 24 in. (76 x 61 cm). This will vary depending on the surface texture you are painting.

Rolling Technique

First paint a narrow vertical strip down one corner with a small brush, then roll in diagonal strokes, working in rectangles of approximately 30 x 24 in. (76 x 61 cm). Repeat vertically to form bands of paint from ceiling to skirting board. Cut into the ceiling and skirting boards with a brush, a short length at a time, just before rolling the next vertical band.

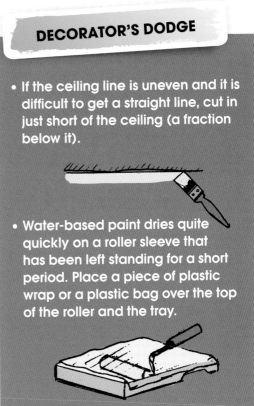

DECORATOR'S DODGE

- If the ceiling line is uneven and it is difficult to get a straight line, cut in just short of the ceiling (a fraction below it).

- Water-based paint dries quite quickly on a roller sleeve that has been left standing for a short period. Place a piece of plastic wrap or a plastic bag over the top of the roller and the tray.

Painting Walls Hung with Vinyl Paper

Most types of vinyl paper can be successfully painted with water-based paint, provided that the vinyl is stuck well, but first check the joints are well stuck down and are not proud (sticking up).

Painting over Joints

Overlapping joints may show more when the vinyl is painted. Follow the step-by-step directions below to help minimize the problem.

1. Coat overlapping joints with undercoat and do not leave thick edges. Let dry thoroughly.
2. Sand down the coated joint—an electric detail sander is handy for this.
3. If the joint is still proud (sticking up), fill to the edge using a fine filler, trying to taper off the filler onto the paper face.
4. When the filler is fully dry, lightly sand, using a medium abrasive wrapped around a block of wood.
5. Coat filled and sanded joints with water-based paint (this will prevent further coats from sinking in) and try to avoid thick edges by rubbing out paint at edges of the coating. Allow to dry before painting.

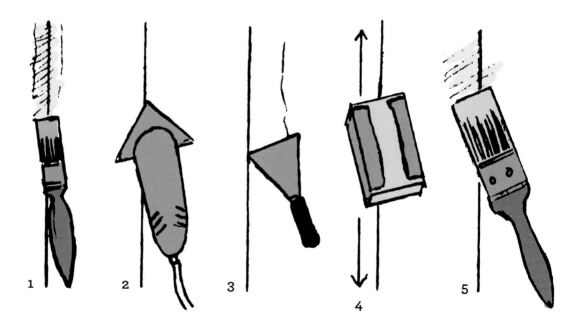

1   2   3   4   5

Securing Loose Joints

If any joints are loose, follow the procedure below:

1. Slightly lift any joints that are loose with a flat-bladed narrow knife, such as a putty knife or chisel knife.

2. With a small brush, apply overlap adhesive behind the loose joint and wipe off any excess paste from the surface of the vinyl.

3. Use a seam roller to roll down the joint and secure the loose joints.

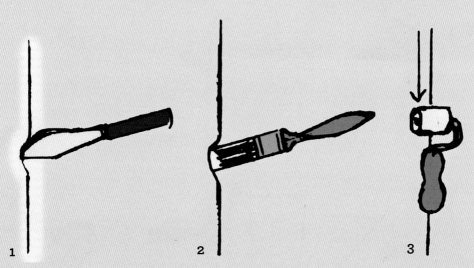

1

2

3

Cleaning Water-Based Paint out of a Roller

Always clean rollers as soon as you have finished using them—there is nothing worse than tackling rollers stiff with dried paint. When leaving a roller under a running tap, make sure that the plug will not slip into the plughole, causing the sink to overflow.

1. Scrape any excess paint from the roller sleeve back into the can using the side edge of a scraper.

2. Place the roller and sleeve under a running cold-water tap. Then run the roller backward and forward along the bottom or side of the sink partly filled with warm water.

3. Apply liquid soap to the roller sleeve—washing up liquid is good for this. Work the soap into a lather. Repeat the rolling and soaping stages.

4. Leave the roller under a cold running tap for a few minutes to clear the remaining traces of paint. Then soak the roller for 15 minutes or more.

5. Spin the roller in a deep sink or an empty bucket to shed excess water. Rub the sleeve dry with a clean cloth.

6. After washing, suspend the roller and sleeve or stand the sleeve on its end. Do not leave the roller on its side, as this can cause a flat area to form on the sleeve pile.

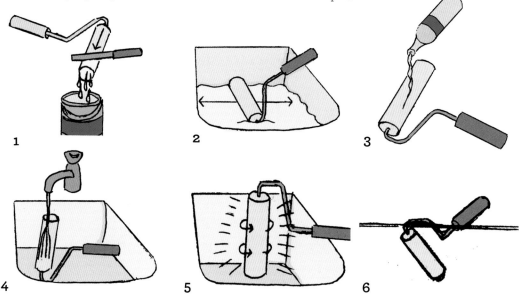

1 2 3

4 5 6

Using a Painting Pad

Although not as quick as a roller, painting pads are easy to use and do not produce a spray.

1. Apply paint to the pad by moving it against the plastic feed roller, set in the paint tray.
2. Use a large pad for big areas. Apply paint in a series of overlapping strips, either vertically or horizontally.
3. Certain types of large pad can be attached to an extension handle.
4. Lesser areas are best painted with smaller pads. It is possible to get pads with an edge guard, which is useful when cutting into internal corners.

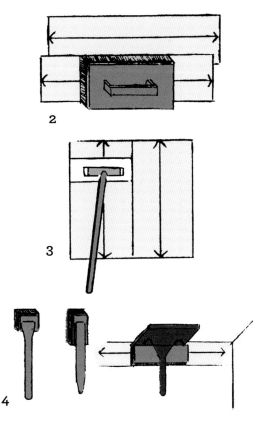

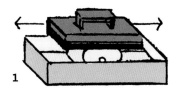

Cleaning a Painting Pad

1. Scrape any excess paint back into the can, using the side edge of a scraper.

2. Fill a tray with water or mineral spirits. Press the pad down into tray and move sideways.

3. Scrape the pad with the side edge of a scraper, then rub the pad out onto a clean rag. Repeat as necessary.

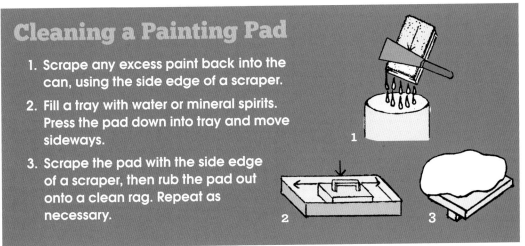

The Order in Which Work Is Carried Out

If a job is to be done smoothly, work needs to be carried out in a certain order.

Painting Order for Rooms and Staircases

1. Paint the ceiling (and any coving).
2. Undercoat the woodwork or at least the edges of the woodwork (where the edges meet the wall). **Note:** If the walls are to be painted, it is not necessary to cut in the woodwork (see page 99); in fact paint onto the wall slightly but do not leave thick lines of paint. "Feather off" with the side of a dry brush.
3. Paint the walls; it is best to cut in reasonably, but not precisely, to previously coated undercoated woodwork.
4. Finish the woodwork (gloss etc.), cutting into the walls.

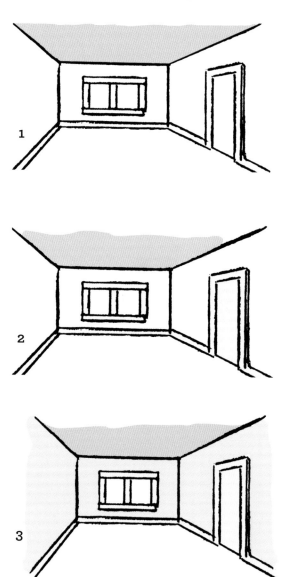

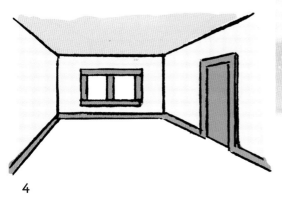

4

Note: The above operations need not be done on separate days, and it may be quicker to combine jobs, in the following ways:
- Combine step 1 (paint or paper ceiling) with step 2 (undercoating woodwork)
- Combine step 3 (paint walls) with step 4 (finish woodwork), or at least *the* woodwork other than the edges that come against the painted walls.

Note: Although not regarded by professional decorators as a very good method, some amateurs prefer to gloss the woodwork before painting the walls. They feel that it is easier to wipe off stray matte from dry gloss than it is to wipe off stray gloss from dry matte. The disadvantage of this method is that any matte left on the gloss does bond very well to the gloss, and this can lead to peeling. Also, care has to be taken to make sure skirting boards and windowsills are not affected by "roller drizzle."

Painting and Wallpapering Order for Rooms and Staircases

1. Strip off existing wallpaper if required, clean down walls, fill, sand, and size coat.
2. Paint or hang paper to ceiling.
3. Hang lining paper horizontally if necessary (see Hanging Lining Paper, page 155).
4. Undercoat the woodwork, or at least the edges that meet the walls. Overlap onto the walls slightly.
5. Gloss the woodwork, or at least the edges that meet the walls, overlapping onto the walls slightly. Paint the inner areas such as the doors and window sections.
6. Hang the wallpaper.

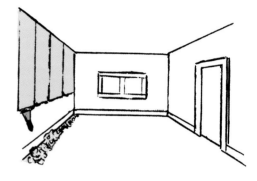

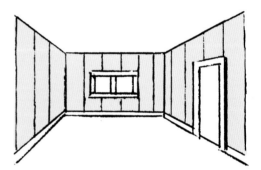

Order of Painting when Hanging Woodchip or Anaglypta

The procedure is slightly different than when hanging wallpaper.

1. Hang the woodchip or anaglypta.
2. Undercoat the woodwork, painting slightly onto the woodchip, and allow paint to dry.
3. Paint the woodchip or anaglypta, painting very slightly onto the undercoated woodwork and wiping off any excess paint.
4. When the paint is dry, gloss the woodwork, cutting into the walls.

Cutting In Techniques

Trades people tend to use a small 1½ in. (39 mm) brush to cut in straight lines, although DIY workers tend to use either a 1 in. (26 mm) or a ½ in. (13 mm) brush. The problem with using a smaller brush is that it does not hold as much paint, so gives a slower paint application rate. Either way, follow these step-by-step instructions:

1. Load the brush fairly generously with paint.
2. Apply quite a heavy band of paint near the area to be cut in.
3. Drag the paint toward the cutting-in line.
4. Use the flat edge of the bristle to cut in, OR turn the brush sideways to cut in.

DECORATOR'S DODGE

- To save cutting in, if the ceiling and walls are to be painted, overlap slightly onto the walls when painting the ceiling. If the walls and woodwork are to be painted, overlap the undercoat slightly onto the walls before painting the walls.

- If you are unlucky enough to get paint onto adjacent surfaces when cutting in, wrap a slightly damp rag around a scraper blade and drag the scraper and rag along the surface, close to the cutting in.

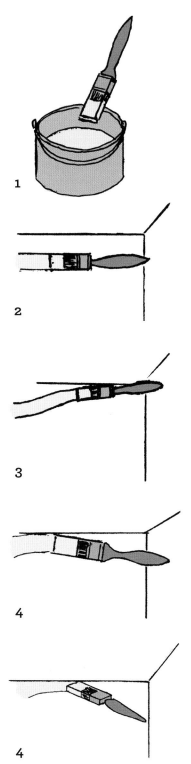

1

2

3

4

4

Using a Paint Shield

It is possible to buy commercial paint shields, but you can improvise using small pieces of thick card.

Note: Wipe surplus paint off the paint shield regularly.

A commercial paint shield

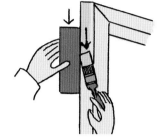

Using an edge shield

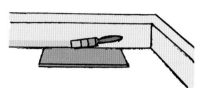

Using a piece of card in the gap below the skirting

Masking Off

If you can't cut in very well, mask off where possible.

Windows

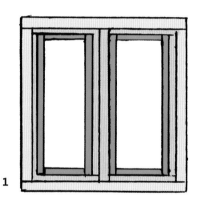

1. Stick 1-in. (2.5-cm) wide masking tape to the glass, as close to the window sections as possible.
2. Leave the tape in position until the paint has initially dried, but is still soft. Peel the tape off carefully at an angle and across itself, away from the window sections.
3. Scrape off any traces of paint on the glass with a razor blade scraper.

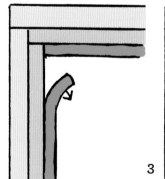

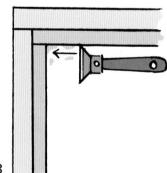

Note: Do not leave the tape on for long periods, as it may become difficult to remove; it could leave ragged edges as it pulls paint off.

DECORATOR'S DODGE
It is a good idea to wear disposable plastic gloves when removing the masking tape, because the tape may have wet paint on it.

Walls

You may need to mask walls where two colors are going to be used very close together, for instance at wall divisions or dados.

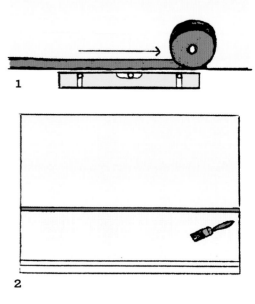

1. Paint the upper wall area. When fully dry, mark out a horizontal line using either a straight edge and pencil, or a chalk line and chalk. Use a level to check the horizontal position. Stick masking tape gently up to the horizontal line.

2. Paint the lower section of the wall. Avoid brushing upward toward the tape. This can cause paint to creep under the tape.

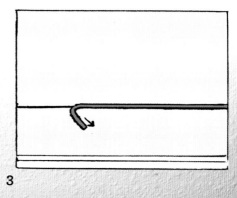

3. Peel the tape off slowly and gently at a downward angle, back upon itself, and before the paint on the lower section of the wall is completely dry.

Equipment with Cutting In Aids

Rollers: It is possible to buy paint rollers with shields, sometimes called edge rollers. These have a plastic guard at one side of the roller. The guard can be moved out of the way using a lever action on the handle.

Painting pads: Some paint pads have an edge shield, which can be pressed against the surface at right angles to the surface being painted. In addition, some pads have small wheels to help the shield run across the surface.

Angled brushes: Small brushes, about ½ in. (13 mm), can be obtained with a "clipped" angled edge to assist when cutting in.

Lining fitches: Small flat fitches with an angled tip can be used for cutting in. They are used against a straight edge, which is set slightly off the surface on two blocks. Two matchboxes taped to either end of a straight flat lath can make a makeshift straight edge.

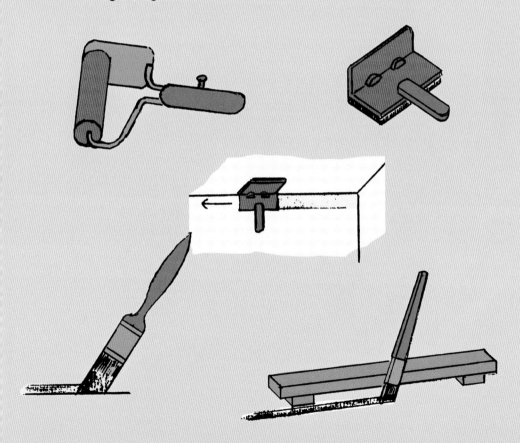

Tools Needed for Texture Painting

Texture paint (or texturing paint) comes either ready-mixed or as a fine powder, which is mixed up to a working consistency with water. It does, however, require a few specialist tools.

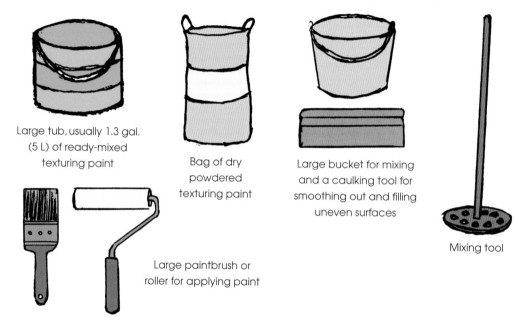

Large tub, usually 1.3 gal. (5 L) of ready-mixed texturing paint

Bag of dry powdered texturing paint

Large bucket for mixing and a caulking tool for smoothing out and filling uneven surfaces

Mixing tool

Large paintbrush or roller for applying paint

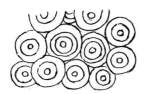

Rubber stippler used for "random swirl" pattern

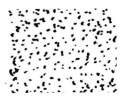
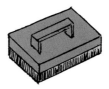

Stippling tool with fine rubber bristles used for stippling a fine texture

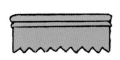

Plastic comb used for patterns with lines

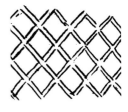

Foam rubber roller with diamond pattern creates a diamond effect

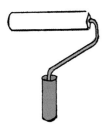

Smooth plastic roller creates a bark effect

Sponge with plastic bag wrapped around it creates a "broken leather" effect

Applying Texture Paint

Always make sure before you start texturing that you have enough texture paint for the whole job. Like any other painting job, there is a particular order to the work in hand.

1. Lay in a narrow band of paint across the surface (where possible across the light source) about 2 x 3 ft. (61 x 91 cm).
2. Texture this band, leaving a 1 in. (25 mm) area not textured at the outer edge.
3. Lay in a second band of paint, carefully working into the non-textured narrow strip of the first band.
4. Texture the second laid-in band, and continue in bands across the surface.
5. Finish the edges of the ceiling by dragging a narrow brush along the edge, creating a smooth strip to give a finished look.
6. At internal corners of walls, try to imitate the surface texture, using a sponge or a small brush to stipple in and texture.

DECORATOR'S DODGE
To keep texturing tools soft for short periods, wrap in damp plastic bags and place in an empty bucket.

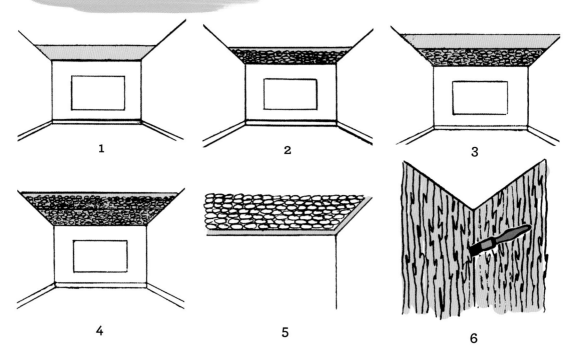

1 2 3

4 5 6

Tools Needed for Applying Creative Paint and Glaze Effects

"Broken color" refers to the technique of applying one color (or colors) on top of another (referred to as the background or ground color), then working on the top color with anything that will cause the background to show through the top coat.

1. **Stippling brush** Can have either hair or rubber filaments. Used to produce a fine or a medium texture
2. **Flogger** Used to produce graining effects
3. **Dragging brush** Used for effects such as wood grain
4. **Softener** Used to soften off broken color effects
5. **Round stenciling** brush and typical stencil mask
6. **Metal comb** Used to create lines and grain effects

7. **Fitch** Used for detailed work
8. **Lining fitch** Used for painting straight lines

Note: A makeshift comb can be cut from a plastic milk bottle. A soft dust brush can double up as softening brush, although not as effectively as an expensive badger softener.

9. **Natural sponge** Used for sponging color on or off
10. **Lint-free rag** Used for wiping or dabbing paint or glaze
11. **Plastic bag** Used for "bagging" effects

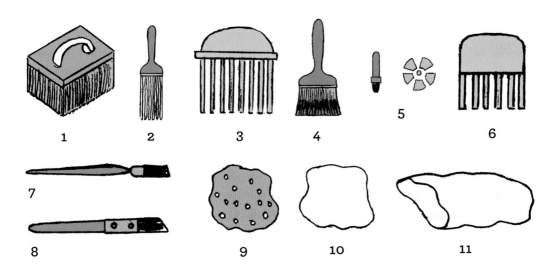

Applying Creative Paint and Glaze Effects

Basic Broken-Color Technique

Oil-based glaze with color stain added (to make a semi-transparent coating) is applied onto a dry, previously coated surface (background color). Then while the glaze color is still wet (known as "the open time") it is worked on with one of the tools (see page 107) to produce a broken-color effect.

Note: It is possible to get a water-based glaze coat, but the wet time (open time) may not be as long as the oil-based variety.

Different Types of Broken-Color Effects

Stippling

1. The ground color, usually eggshell finish, is applied to the surface and allowed to dry.
2. The semi-transparent glaze coat with stainers added is applied over the ground color.
3. The applied glaze coat is lightly stippled with a short-haired stippler, leaving an open dappled effect.

Notes: Only lay in a small amount of glaze coat, which will stay "open" (wet) long enough to be worked on with the stippling brush.

The stippling brush should be used lightly and evenly to produce a uniform pattern.

A heavier stippling pattern can be obtained by using a rubber bristled texturing brush.

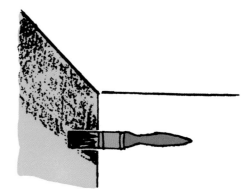

1

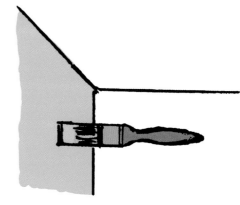

2

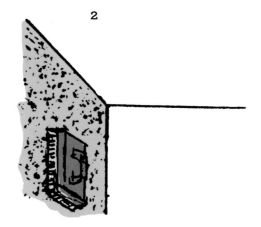

3

Stippling and Wiping

This effect is used to highlight ornamental surfaces, such as moldings.

1. A stained glaze coat is applied over a dry ground coat. For best results, the ground coat should be white.
2. The glaze coat is stippled.
3. The highlights (tops) of the ornament are wiped clean of glaze coat using a rag wrapped around the thumb.

1

2

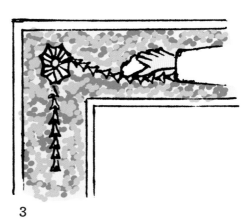

3

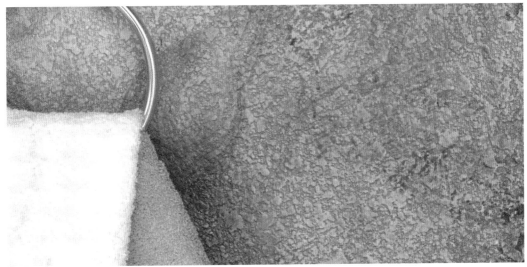

Ragging

To achieve this effect, a rag is dabbed over the surface of the second color.

1. Pour the color to be used for ragging into a roller tray.
2. Dip a lint-free crumpled rag into the paint and dab out the thick paint onto the roller-loading area. Wear disposable gloves.
3. Dab the rag onto the previously coated surface (usually a contrasting color) as evenly as possible. Reload the rag regularly.

Note: It is possible to use eggshell finish, satin, or matte paint as an alternative to tinted glaze.

Bagging is a technique similar to ragging except that a plastic bag is used to dab the paint instead of a cloth.

Rag Rolling

During this technique a rag is rolled across the surface of the paint to create an interesting effect.

1. A ground coat is applied and allowed to dry.
2. A glaze coat stained with a contrasting color is added over the ground coat.
3. A length of rolled-up rag is rolled upward across the surface, wiping off the glaze in places to reveal the ground-coat color.

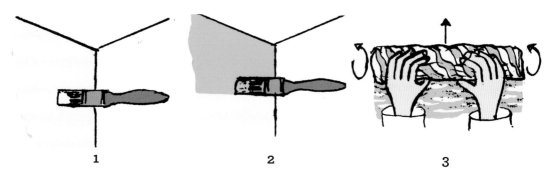

Sponging (Paint On)

1. Dampen a natural sea sponge to allow it to swell up. Squeeze out the water. **Note:** A natural sponge gives a better finish than an artificial one.
2. Load the sponge with paint and dab out the excess on a paint tray.
3. Dab the loaded sponge evenly over the ground coat in a circular manner.

Sponging (Color Off)

Similar to the above, except that stained glaze coat is dabbed off with a sponge to show the ground coat.

Graining

The point of this technique is to produce a wood-colored and wood-grained effect.

1. A wood-colored glaze coat, sometimes called "scumble," is applied over an appropriate dry ground coat: buff for oak, deep pink for mahogany, and fawn for walnut. You can get a ready-made scumble.
2. Dragging: A coarse brush is pulled across the scumble, which leaves a grain-like pattern.
3. Flogging: A special coarse long-bristled brush is pulled across the surface. This produces a finer grain effect than with dragging.

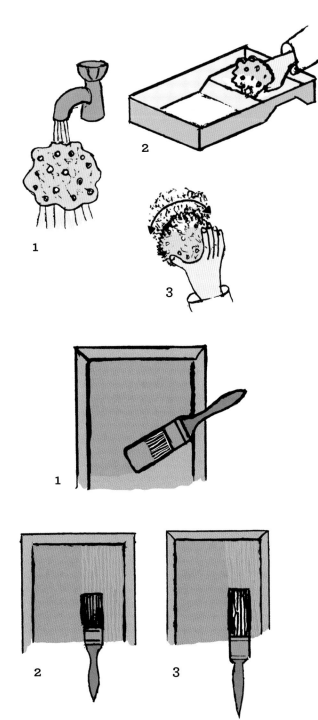

Stenciling

To achieve this effect a cut-out pattern is stipple-painted with a stencil brush (a short-haired round brush with flat ends) using short, even tapping strokes. Stencils can be purchased ready-made, but you can make your own out of firm card or plastic.

Making a Stencil

1. Place a sheet of tracing paper over a design and trace out the pattern.
2. Rub lead pencil over the back of the tracing paper, then draw over the pattern to reproduce the design onto a card of medium thickness (tape the tracing paper to the card).
3. Apply shellac primer to both sides of the card and over the design; allow it to dry.
4. Using a sharp craft knife, cut out the design. **Note:** It is important to leave "ties," which are pieces of card holding the design together.
5. Mark out the positions where the designs are to be placed, using chalk. Place the stencil over the chalk marks.
6. Dip the ends of the stencil brush bristles into the paint and dab out the paint onto a flat piece of wood or a lid. Then dab the brush onto the stencil design, using short, even strokes, and keeping the brush at right angles to the stencil.

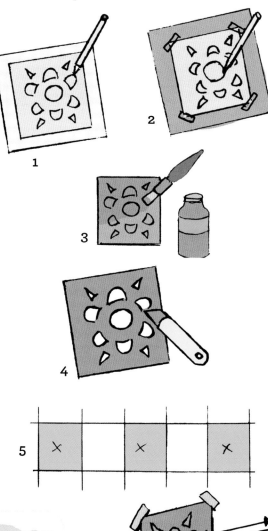

DECORATOR'S DODGE

A makeshift stencil brush can be made by tightly wrapping the bristles of a small brush with masking tape, leaving the tips protruding.

Paint Problems and Remedies

Bits in Paint Finish

Causes
- Paint contaminated with grit or dust from the surface being painted
- Small pieces of broken paint skin

Prevention
Make sure that the surface to be painted is dusted off and wiped clean with a "tack cloth," or a lint-free rag moistened slightly with mineral spirits. If paint is contaminated with bits, strain the paint through a stretched pair of pantyhose or old kitchen sifter (see Straining Paint, page 72).

Remedy
Flat down the surface and repaint.

Brush Marks and Tram Lines (or Ladders)

Causes
- Tram lines—inadequate brush work, missing sections when laying off the paint and leaving areas, showing cross laying off beneath
- Ropey brush marks—heavy brush work and brushing out paint beyond the normal flow-out time

Prevention
Pay more attention to the laying off technique (see page 75). Do not overbrush.

Remedy
Flat down the surface or remove faulty paint finish.

to warm up a room before glossing, since this speeds up the check time.

Remedy

Wait until the paint surface is fully dry, then "flat down" with abrasive or remove the paint and start again.

Paint "Misses" and "Grinning"

Causes

- Misses—uneven application and possibly not all painted
- Grinning—paint applied too thinly in places, allowing the surface underneath to show through

Prevention

Apply enough paint evenly, with sufficient crossing and laying-off brush strokes. Always look across the painted surface, against the light if possible.

Remedy

Leave paint to dry, then flat down and repaint.

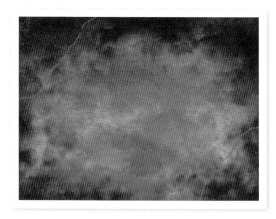

Runs, Sags, Curtains

Causes

- Application of too much paint, underbrushing, or overbrushing
- Sometimes cold conditions can cause runs, as the paint does not check (initially dry) as quickly
- Not keeping a flowing "wet edge" (working edge) to the paint during application

Prevention

Try to apply as much paint as will check (initially dry) within a reasonable time. Do not overload the surface. Do not try to brush the paint out beyond its check time as this can cause it to roll up on itself and run. Try

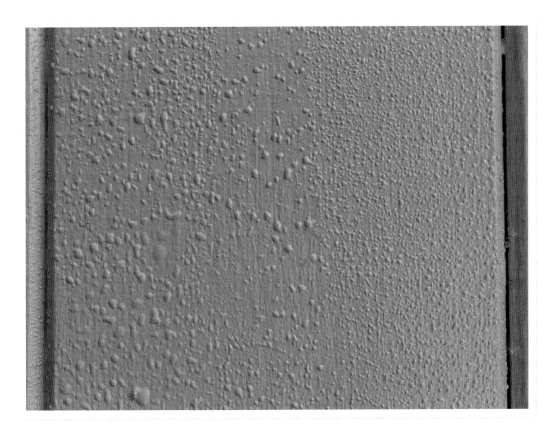

Blisters (Most Common on Gloss Paint)

Causes

- Moisture, solvents, or resin trapped beneath a paint film, not making sure that a surface is dry or painting in damp conditions, or not stirring the paint up sufficiently
- Not treating resinous areas, such as knots, before painting

Prevention

Always make sure that the surface to be painted is fully dry, and do not paint in damp conditions. Treat resinous knots with 1–2 coats of shellac primer and allow to dry before painting. Stir paint thoroughly before use.

Remedy

The best way is to remove the paint and start again, but sometimes an isolated blister can be scraped, filled, and sanded, then repainted.

Cissing and Fretting

Description

Where paint or varnish pulls away from the paint beneath and forms a series of semi-circular areas.

Causes

- Incompatibility between coatings—i.e., water-based paint over an unflattened gloss paint
- Grease or oil on the surface
- Certain household polishes can cause cissing

Prevention

Clean surfaces prior to painting and "flat down" gloss paint.

Remedy

Wipe off the paint if it is still wet and use abrasives on the surface, then wipe with rag and mineral spirits; dry off before repainting. If affected paint is dry, flat down thoroughly, wash with detergent, and repaint.

Blooming

Description

Where gloss varnish or gloss paint dries milky, looking dull and flat.

Causes

- Often caused by cold damp conditions such as condensation, steam, or fog
- Sometimes from the fumes of solvents, gas, or thinners such as mineral spirits, which were not thoroughly mixed into the paint

Prevention

Avoid painting in damp conditions, steam, etc.

Remedy

Flat down and allow the surface to dry out thoroughly before recoating. Sometimes slight blooming can be removed by rubbing surface with soapy water.

Fading and Discoloration

Causes

- Strong sunlight, alkaline salts, atmospheric pollution, coastal atmosphere, sea salts, lack of daylight (yellowing of whites); see also Bleeding, page 24
- Certain pigments fade quite quickly, and are described as "fugitive" to light; e.g., some blues are particularly susceptible

Prevention

Do not use fugitive colors (colors that fade easily) in areas that are exposed to strong sunlight.

Remedy

As above.

Part Four

Hanging Wallpaper

Types of Wallpaper

DIY decorating is not just a simple matter of painting—hanging wallpaper is another decorating task that you might like to tackle on your own. And like paint, wallpaper comes in a confusing array of choices and materials. Getting to grips with the basics is a good place to start.

Lining Paper

A smooth, flat, unfinished paper, lining paper comes in different thickness (or weight) grades:

- Standard weight 200 grade
- Medium weight 400 grade
- Heavyweight 600 grade.

Lining paper rolls come in standard lengths (11 yds./10.05 m), but you can get double-length or even quadruple-length paper. Where a lot of lining is to be done, it can save paper.

Description

Lining paper is used under wallpaper as a smooth "ground." It helps to cover up surface imperfections and to even up the amount of porosity (suction) in a surface. On previously glossed surfaces, it is necessary to hang lining paper (after flatting down the gloss) before hanging vinyl or wallpaper. Lining paper can also be used as a ground when painting ceilings or walls in poor condition.

Special-Purpose Lining Papers

Cotton- or linen-backed lining papers
These can be used over cracked and filled ceilings and walls to help prevent cracks moving and opening up. They are hung with the fabric side to the surface.

Pitch backed lining papers (usually brown) These are coated on one side with a nonporous pitch coating and are used over areas where dampness is a problem. They are hung pitch-side to the surface.

Woodchip

Sometimes called wood ingrain, woodchip is supplied in fine, medium, and heavy textures, and in single-, double-, and quadruple-length rolls. It is ideal for hiding rough and uneven surfaces and is durable when painted.

Standard Patterned Wallpaper

Comes in lightweight, medium weight, and heavyweight qualities, and in matte finish or sheen, flat surfaced or slightly textured. The heavyweights generally need a longer soakage time when pasted, whereas the lightweights may become thin and difficult to handle when soaked. Follow the manufacturer's recommended soakage time, usually given on roll instructions.

Note: Avoid overbrushing matte-finished papers, especially at the joints, as this can cause polishing and shiny streaks on the surface.

Embossed Paper

These papers have a pattern, which is in relief and has depth. They are produced by passing the paper between relief pattern rollers, and are recognized by the hollow texture at the back of the paper. Avoid overbrushing or using a seam roller, as this can flatten the pattern. Often self-finished, although sometimes they need finishing with matte paint, satin, etc.

Duplex paper This heavy-thickness paper is usually two or more papers laminated onto a paper backing. Can hide imperfections.

Anaglypta Hollow-backed, this heavy-thickness paper needs finishing with paint. Needs adequate soakage time when pasted, and is liable to stretch if overbrushed or soaked too long. Hang from the center of the wall, then upward toward the top and downward toward the floor. Durable when painted.

Vinyls

This type of paper consists of a layer of vinyl facing (often fabric) laminated to a paper backing. It can be smooth-faced or slightly textured, and comes in a large range of colored patterns. The material is durable, washable, and reasonably easy to hang. It should not be hung over damp-affected areas, as it is prone to black mildew and lifting from the papered surface. The vinyl will not remain stuck at any overlaps with the vinyl surface. If overlaps are unavoidable, an overlap adhesive should be used (usually supplied in tubes). A good heavy-duty cellulose type adhesive is necessary, or a heavy-duty ready-mixed tub paste.

The face of the vinyl can often be dry-peeled when stripping off, although I would recommend stripping off the backing paper with water, because although it may look like a sound surface to hang new paper over, sometimes the backing paper can lift and blister under the new paper.

Blown vinyl Usually has patterned backgrounds in high or low profile, with colored motif patterns printed on top. These materials can be recognized by their flat back and are easier to paste than embossed papers or anaglypta, and are good to handle and hang. The high-profile patterns are excellent for covering and hiding uneven surfaces, but tend to be a bit soft when it comes to resisting wear and tear. The low profile varieties tend to be less vulnerable. These vinyls become relatively durable after they have hardened up. Because of the vinyl

Because the top of the wall where it meets the ceiling can be uneven, especially if the ceiling dips in places, it is a good idea to start the tile pattern a little down from the ceiling, i.e., with the horizontal grout line away from the ceiling. This gives a better result if there are wall height differences than a full tile pattern line running into the ceiling.

face and the profile, overlapping cannot be done successfully. Blown vinyls can usually be dry-peeled when stripping off. Heavy-duty adhesives are best. **Tip:** Leave painting the vinyl until it has been on for a while, then "freshen up" when redecorating.

Cushion vinyl (includes "tile on the roll") Quite a thick vinyl-faced paper, with a soft cushion finish, which is washable. Heavyweight adhesive is necessary. Avoid overlapping. May require a lining paper to be hung first; in spite of the thickness of the material, imperfections on the surface may show through the paper.

When using tile on the roll papers, it is essential to keep the horizontal lines running true because of the horizontal as well as the vertical lines of the represented tile grout. Using a plumb bob and a level is a good way of checking this.

Washables (vinyl-coated) A cheap and sometimes quite thin paper, which can be difficult to hang—too much or too little

soakage and blisters can form. Too much brushing can result in wrinkles. Keep to the manufacturer's instructions with regard to soakage time. Washables usually will not dry-peel and tend to be difficult.

Wide Fabric-Faced Vinyl and Hessian

These are 54 in. (137 cm) wide or more and are used where overall textures provide the decoration rather than patterns. Sometimes every other length is reversed, to give a more random effect. Mostly used in commercial premises, very often as feature walls.

Due to their width these papers are usually hung by professional decorators. Each length is overlapped by about 2 in. (5 cm), then both the overlap and the piece underneath are cut through with a sharp-bladed knife, using a straight edge to cut against. Then the cut edges are stuck down and butted together, and any surplus paste on the surface wiped off. Heavy-duty, ready-mixed tub paste is recommended, which is either applied to the wall surface or the back

of the material, depending on whether the woven face is fabric- or paper-backed (follow the manufacturer's instructions).

Woodgrain-Effect Papers

These papers have either a pattern representing wood—the grain effect either slightly embossed and having a texture—or are printed matte with a smooth finish. Some patterns represent boards or planking. The smooth-faced variety may require the surface to be first hung with lining paper. Cellulose-type adhesives are usually used with these papers.

Stone- and Brick-Effect Papers

These can vary from smooth-faced photographically produced paper, to quite thick, slightly embossed effects.

DECORATOR'S DODGE
When stripping paper, first rub the surface with either a coarse abrasive or a wire brush, to help to "open up" the washable surface and make it more porous.

Traditionally often used on fireplace walls or dado areas (lower wall sections) or as feature areas, the thicker varieties require heavyweight adhesives.

Flock Papers

The patterns of flock paper are formed by a raised pile on a colored paper background. Originally the pile would be silk, but nowadays the pile is usually synthetic fibers; consequently these papers are not as expensive as they used to be. Flock paper requires careful handling when pasting and hanging, paste on the face of the paper can be difficult to remove and can spoil the raised pile pattern. Care should be taken not to flatten the pile at the seams if using a seam roller. A heavy-duty adhesive should be used, and it is best to first hang lining paper on the walls.

Moiré

Papers that have a watered-silk effect (often in the background, behind the pattern) are produced by fine embossing and are sometimes supplied as vinyl. Care should be taken to ensure that the adhesive is kept off the face of the paper, as it can be difficult to remove from the finely embossed background. If your walls are old and imperfect, line with lining paper first.

Striped Papers

Supplied as standard wallpaper, vinyl, blown vinyl, embossed paper, anaglypta, washable, moiré, and flock papers. The striped patterns can vary in width of stripe from thin pinstripes to wide decorated stripes.

Sometimes the stripes alternate between other patterns. A stripe pattern can make a room feel taller, but a bold stripe can be dominating and have the effect of enclosing a room.

Great care needs to be taken to hang stripes vertically straight, as any slightly crooked lengths are exaggerated by the stripe. If vertical corners of a room are slanted, stripes are best avoided, as it will show up the imperfections.

Lincrusta (Walton)

A thick, low-relief material produced by oxidized linseed oil to produce a hard putty-like face. Supplied in either panels (with separate borders) or in rolls, these can have a decorative finish or be a plain buff color, which has to be stained and varnished or painted. Many of the patterns are wood effects, but there are a number of other patterns such as tiles, leather effects, and ornamental decorations. These materials require skill to handle and hang, and may be best hung by a professional decorator.

DECORATOR'S DODGE
Before hanging Lincrusta, it helps if you first soak each piece to be hung with warm water; this makes the material more pliable, flexible, and supple. A very strong adhesive, such as rubber glue, is necessary.

Wallpaper Roll Symbols and Instructions

The following information is usually displayed on the wallpaper roll label: pattern number, batch number (or lot number), pattern design name, and color. There may well be a number of other symbols, some of which are shown below.

Note: Wallpaper is manufactured in batches, so each batch may vary slightly. Therefore it is important to buy wallpaper with the same batch number, as well as pattern number.

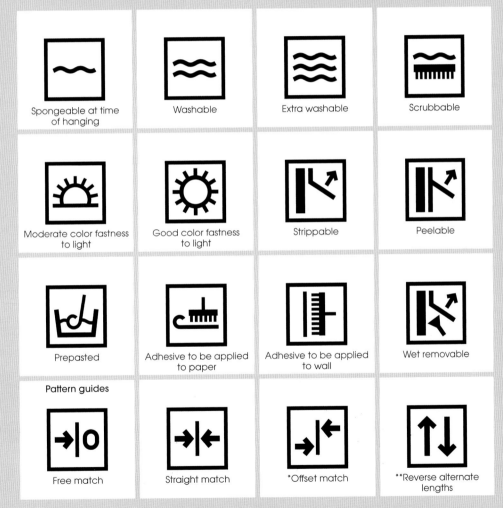

Spongeable at time of hanging	Washable	Extra washable	Scrubbable
Moderate color fastness to light	Good color fastness to light	Strippable	Peelable
Prepasted	Adhesive to be applied to paper	Adhesive to be applied to wall	Wet removable

Pattern guides

Free match	Straight match	*Offset match	**Reverse alternate lengths

* Creates an alternating top to lengths of paper: i.e., lengths 1 and 3 are the same pattern, and 2 and 4 have a different section of pattern opposite.
** Turn every other length upside down to create a random effect. Usually the size of the pattern repeat is shown, e.g., repeat 64/32 cm.

Wallpaper Patterns – Hanging Types

There are thousands of different patterns and dozens of different types, but from the point of view of hanging wallpaper, the patterns fall into four hanging methods.

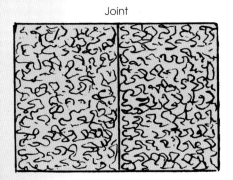

Joint

Plain Patterns with No Match

These wallpapers tend to have textures and some have all-over patterns. The paper can be hung at random and can also be described as free-match or random-match.

Note: To obtain an even, more random effect, some paper instructions advice hanging every other length upside down.

Patterns with a Straight Through Match

Patterns that line up horizontally and match at the edge of the paper fall into this category.

Note: Pattern at the top of each length is identical. Lengths of paper are cut with the same pattern in line at the top of each length.

Joint   Joint

Patterns with a Drop Repeat and Alternating Top

Every other length has a different pattern at the top of each length hung: for instance 1, 3, and 5 have one type of pattern top, whereas lengths 2, 4, and 6 are another type of pattern top.

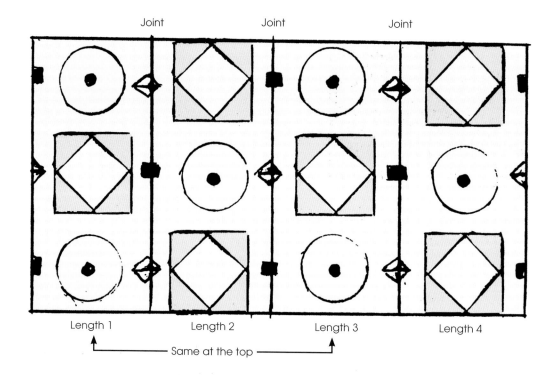

Joint   Joint   Joint

Length 1   Length 2   Length 3   Length 4

↑————— Same at the top —————↑

DECORATOR'S DODGE

A good method when marking out where the lengths should go around a room is to mark a cross on the wall at every other length, then mark a cross on the back of every second roll used (see opposite). Then, continue using further sets of two rolls for remaining lengths.

Note: To avoid confusion while hanging the paper, it is a good idea to mark lengths cut off the marked alternating roll, and place them in a separate position to the unmarked lengths (see diagram opposite).

Note: To save paper, it is a good idea to cut lengths from alternate rolls of paper: for example, lengths 1, 3, and 5 from one roll and lengths 2, 4, and 6 from another roll. See an example of "marking out" a room for an alternating pattern below.

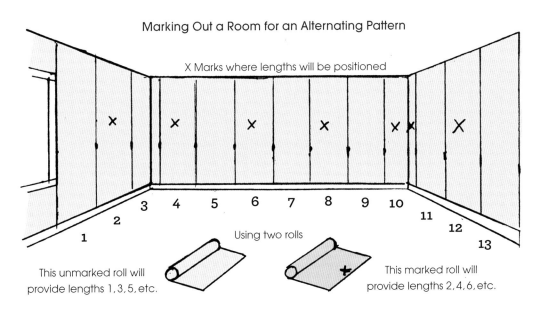

Marking Out a Room for an Alternating Pattern

X Marks where lengths will be positioned

Using two rolls

This unmarked roll will provide lengths 1, 3, 5, etc.

This marked roll will provide lengths 2, 4, 6, etc.

Patterns with No Paper Edge Match, but Which Have to Be Lined Up Horizontally

Some stripe patterns, for instance, which have no edge match, may have a pattern motif between the stripes that has to be lined up horizontally.

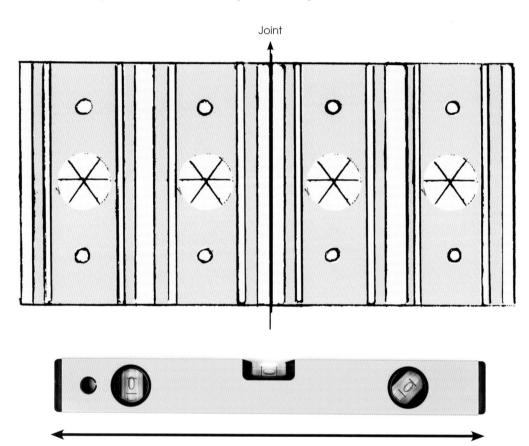

Pattern between stripes has to be lined up horizontally by eye and checked with a horizontal level

Preparing Surfaces for Wallpaper

Before we actually discuss which surfaces can be wallpapered, it is important to remember that there are some surfaces that are unsuitable or difficult to cover with paper.

Surfaces Unsuitable for Wallpaper

- Bricks, concrete sections, and textured surfaces all have irregular surfaces and would look uneven and terrible if papered.

- Glazed tiles, glass panels, glass, and metal all have smooth, nonporous surfaces, which make it difficult for an adhesive to stick, and the paste would have to dry out through the paper, which could mark the face.

- Although it is possible to hang paper on new plaster, it is not a good idea as the paste is sucked into the surface, and when stuck paper bonds and laminates with the plaster, it makes it very difficult to remove later when trying to strip it off.

Surfaces That Are Difficult to Paper

- Plasterboard, fiberboard, and wood are all very porous and tend to suck in the adhesive. Thorough size-coating is necessary, which must be allowed to dry before paper-hanging. When hanging heavyweight papers, it may be necessary to first hang lining paper.

- Gloss painted surfaces are nonporous and do not provide a good surface for the adhesive to stick to (see page 134).

Preparing Painted Surfaces for Wallpaper

Emulsion Painted Surfaces

Matte-painted surfaces and surfaces with a slight sheen, such as satin, may pose a problem, as they may not be sound (stuck thoroughly to the surface) and can, if loose, come away on the back of the paper, bringing the paper off. This can happen when hanging heavyweight paper with an extra strong adhesive (the adhesive can work on the paint, loosening it).

1. Always wash the surface, and while wet, scrub it and note whether any areas show signs of lifting.
2. Apply an even coat of size. Note whether the size coat causes the paint to come away as it dries out.
3. Should you be unfortunate and the paint shows signs of lifting and loosening, scrape off these areas while wet, then wash off the size coat.
4. Allow the surface to dry out thoroughly, then scrape and sand all loose areas and dust off.
5. Apply a primer sealer to the whole area, and allow plenty of time (usually a day) for it to dry out.
6. When the primer is dry, hang a lining paper the opposite way to that which the wallpaper is to be hung (for instance, on walls hang the lining paper horizontally).

Note: Do not apply a size coat on top of the sealer, as this just sits on top of the painted surface and does not do much good.

7. Allow lining paper plenty of time to dry out (as it is now on a nonporous surface) before hanging the wallpaper.

> **DECORATOR'S DODGE**
> A useful test to see if a paint surface is sound (although not completely foolproof) is to hang a small rectangle of wallpaper first, and allow it to dry out. If it remains stuck and then strips off without loosening the painted surface, this is some indication that the paint is not loose (or at least not that part of the surface).

Whitening and Size-Bound Distemper

These types of surfaces are loose and powdery, and should be completely removed where possible by wetting, scraping, and scrubbing off. Ceiling and frieze areas, in particular at old properties, are sometimes covered in this material. When clean, apply a size coat and allow to dry thoroughly. Any areas that will not scrub off should be scraped, sanded, and size-coated. When dry, apply a sealer coat to these areas.

Removing Whitening and Size-Bound Distemper

1. Wet in a strip at a time.
2. Scrub off as much whitening or distemper as possible.
3. Change the washing water frequently.
4. Scrape off any remaining thick areas while wet.

Safety note: Wear protective goggles.

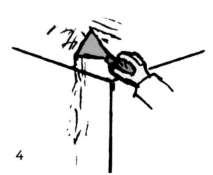

DECORATOR'S DODGE
It is a good idea to spread a double layer of newspapers over drop cloths on the floor when scraping off distemper and water paint. Once you have finished you simply bundle the mess away in the newspaper.

Oil-Bound Distemper and Oil-Bound Water Paint

These surfaces will not scrub off, and can cause a problem when they are "shelling" (flaking off). They may require thorough scraping and sanding and, in some cases, filling the edges of flaking areas followed by further light sanding. Then "fasten down" by sealing with a primer sealer and hang lining paper if necessary.

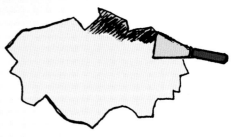

Fill the edges of a scraped area of loose oil-bound water paint

Gloss Painted Surfaces

Any loose areas of this type of surface should be scraped, filled, and sanded. Otherwise the whole surface requires thorough "flatting down," which can be done dry with an electric orbital sander or manually (protective mask and goggles are necessary). It can also be "flatted" using wet-and-dry abrasive paper and water, with the abrasive wrapped around a sanding block, followed by removing surface dust and residue thoroughly. It is necessary to hang lining paper to the flatted surface (cross line in the opposite direction to the following wallpaper). **Note:** Do not apply a size coat.

Allow plenty of time for the lining paper to dry out (at least a day) before hanging the wallpaper.

Preparing Previously Papered Surfaces for Wallpaper

It is best to strip off old wallpaper even if it appears to be sound (stuck well). Paper that seems sound can lift off the surface, spring away at the joints, and blister when the newly pasted wallpaper is applied. Vinyl papers that "dry peel," leaving a backing paper that looks like lining paper, are best fully stripped because this is not a suitable surface and often blisters and lifts off beneath the new wallpaper, causing problems.

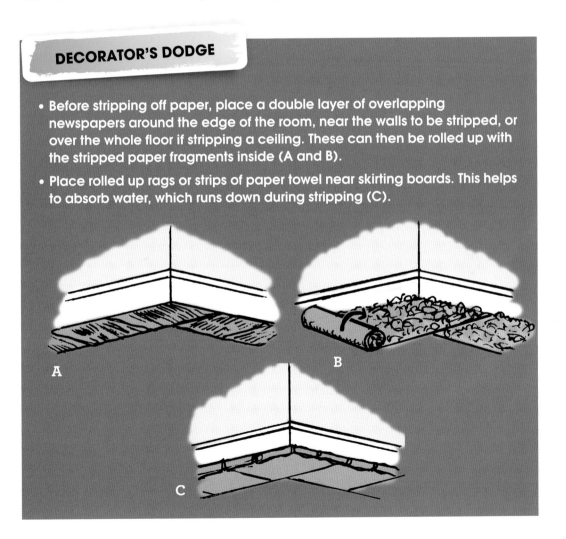

DECORATOR'S DODGE

- Before stripping off paper, place a double layer of overlapping newspapers around the edge of the room, near the walls to be stripped, or over the whole floor if stripping a ceiling. These can then be rolled up with the stripped paper fragments inside (A and B).

- Place rolled up rags or strips of paper towel near skirting boards. This helps to absorb water, which runs down during stripping (C).

Tips When Using a Steam Stripper

- Do not overfill the stripper—this can result in the steam plate spitting scalding hot water.

- Remember to check that the steam stripper does not boil dry, as this can damage the heating elements or the thermostat. Not many steam strippers have a water level gauge, so you have to check how full the level is by feeling the weight of the stripper.

- If wallpaper is difficult to remove, first use a perforator (a device that makes small holes in the paper) allowing the steam to penetrate better.

- Do not leave the steam plate on the wall very long (no more than about 15 seconds). If you can hear slight cracking sounds, beware; it usually means loose plaster.

- Turn off the electricity when working near switches and sockets.

- It is often quicker to boil a couple of kettles to fill the steam stripper, or fill with hot water from the tap, rather than use the stripper to heat the water.

- It is best to wet in and scrub down (using an old flat brush) following steam stripping, while the old size coat is still soft. Time can be saved by doing this to the first stripped area, while waiting for the kettle or steam stripper to boil.

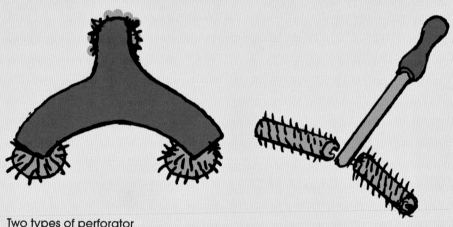

Two types of perforator

Stripping Wallpaper Manually (the Traditional Way)

Safety note: When stripping using water near light switches and sockets, turn off the electricity.

First try to remove any dry, loose paper before wetting in the walls with a flat brush and cold water—just enough to stay wet. Repeat the wetting sequence at least two or three times, and keep the surface wet. It is possible to buy "wetting agents" that can be added to the water to help it soak into the paper.

DECORATOR'S DODGE

- While stripping the first, second, and third walls, keep breaking off to wet in all the walls again. This prevents the water from drying out on the paper before you can get to it.

- Place a piece of soft rag over the end of the stripping knife handle to protect the palm of your hand.

- Stripping water can be made more effective by adding a small amount of acetic acid (vinegar) to hot water or by adding liquid soap, which keeps the water on the surface longer.

- If the wallpaper to be stripped has a nonporous face, such as vinyl-coated washable paper, open up the surface with a wire brush or rub with a coarse house brick, before either wetting or steaming.

- As each wall (or ceiling) is stripped, wet in the wall once again (with warm water) and, using an old flat brush, scrub from the top of the wall downward. This will remove any remnants of old paste and size, and wash off small particles of wallpaper, saving a lot of rubbing down later.

Stripping Wallpaper Using a Steam Stripper

Stripping can be quicker and easier with a steam stripper, and these can be rented from some DIY superstores and tool rental shops. They can vary in size and type, but mostly consist of a water-boiling tank that produces steam, which flows through a hose to a steam plate. There are also smaller, handheld steam strippers that heat the water and are handy for getting into confined spaces.

Stripping Walls

Steam rises, so start at the bottom of the wall and place the steam stripper plate in a horizontal position, parallel with the skirting board. Then work in strips across the wall, right to left if right-handed. Hold the steam plate on the wall for no more than 15 seconds or you may crack off the plaster. Strip off sections where the plate has just been steaming. Work horizontally right across the wall.

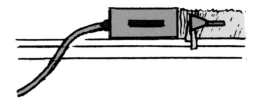

Next, place the steam plate vertically above the stripped area and carry on across the wall from right to left, repeat this upward toward the ceiling.

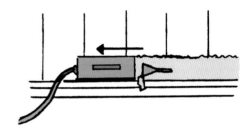

Stripping Ceiling and Walls

Strip the walls first; this allows the steam to rise up and work on the ceiling. If the ceiling is not to be stripped, run a sharp-bladed knife just a fraction below the ceiling and wall corner angle.

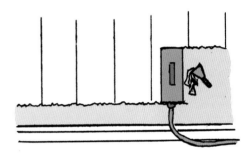

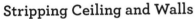

DECORATOR'S DODGE

It is a good idea when steam-stripping ceilings to wear a peaked cap to protect your face from any hot water which may drip. A long-sleeved shirt will also protect your arms.

Preparing Stripped Surfaces for Paper-Hanging

1. All traces of old wallpaper, paste, and old size should be removed by scrubbing with warm water.
2. When dry, sand the surface to get rid of any remaining small fragments of paper, etc.
3. Rake out cracks and apply filler. Fill any surface irregularities. When dry, sand filled areas using a fine to medium abrasive wrapped around a block of wood.
4. Apply a size coat unless the surface is nonporous, such as gloss paint. (Many wallpapers and ceiling papers come away from the surface because they were not sized.)

Note: Size coat used to refer to glue size, which is used beneath some LAP and dextrin-based pastes, but these days size coat is also used for cellulose-based pastes.

DECORATOR'S DODGE
When checking the surface for irregularities, surface imperfections can be highlighted using a low level light such as a table lamp on a cable extension.

Measuring Up for Wallpaper

Square Area Method

Measure the height of the room and the total length around the room (perimeter), or the length of one wall if you are just papering one wall. Do not deduct doors and windows unless there are big areas of windows. Multiply the perimeter of the room by the height to get the total surface area; divide this area by the area of a roll of wallpaper to get the number of rolls needed for the room.

For example: The area of a roll of wallpaper is roughly 33 ft. × 1.8 ft. = 59.4 sq. ft. (or 10 m × 52 cm = 5.2 m²). So divide the area of the room (x sq. ft. or x m²) by 59.4 sq. ft. (5.2 m²) to get the number of rolls.

Measuring ceilings

A convenient way to measure up for a ceiling is to measure the floor (length × width) and divide the total ceiling surface area by the area of a roll of wallpaper.

Rule of Thumb Method

Another, simpler way to measure is to use what I call the rule of thumb method.

1. Measure the height of the room, then divide the length of the roll of wallpaper by the height of the room measurement to find out how many lengths can be cut from a roll. Don't forget to add a couple of inches at top and bottom of the room height to allow for paper-cutting waste and pattern matching.

2. Then, using a short piece of wallpaper roll as a tape measure, mark out the widths needed from the decided starting position. As you mark off the widths around the room, count them up—one, two, three, and so on—to show where the rolls will come. For instance, if you have found that you can get three lengths at 10 ft. (3 m) each from a roll, then every time you mark off three widths of paper, you know that it will each be a roll of paper.

This method is particularly useful for helping you decide where you will start papering. **Note:** It may be convenient to work out a different starting position depending on the room.

DECORATOR'S DODGE
- Sometimes it is possible to count up the existing wallpaper widths of a room to save marking out when measuring.

- For large repeat patterns, add one extra roll in every three rolls, or add the height of the pattern repeat to each length of paper.

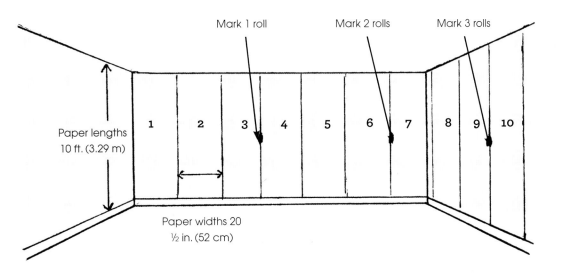

Mark 1 roll   Mark 2 rolls   Mark 3 rolls

Paper lengths
10 ft. (3.29 m)

1 2 3 4 5 6 7 8 9 10

Paper widths 20
½ in. (52 cm)

Rule of Thumb Method—Ceilings

Measure the width of the room and decide how many lengths you can get from the roll at the room width. Next, mark out how many paper widths you can get into the length of the room.

Here it will take 7 widths of paper and it is possible to get 3 lengths of paper from a roll. So it will take just over 2 rolls for the ceiling.

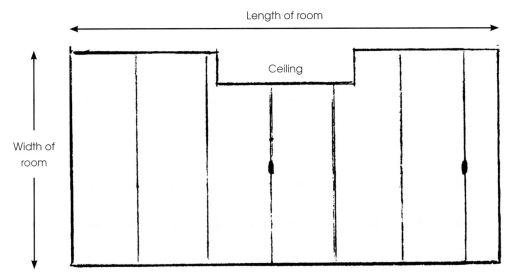

Length of room

Ceiling

Width of
room

Darker marks on ceiling show where each roll comes to.

Measuring Staircases (Landing and Halls)

Because there are so many different wall heights, it is best to measure each different height separately, and weigh up how many paper widths can be obtained at various heights.

Where the height of the wall is about 9 ft. (3 m), you should get three lengths to the roll. Where the height of the wall is approximately 14–15 ft. (4.2–4.5 m), you will only get two lengths to the roll.

If you are not happy calculating the measurements and area, then you can get a rough guide from a wallpaper calculating chart (opposite). For large pattern repeats, add 1 extra roll in every 3 rolls. Or add the size of the wallpaper pattern repeat onto the paper length (room height measurement).

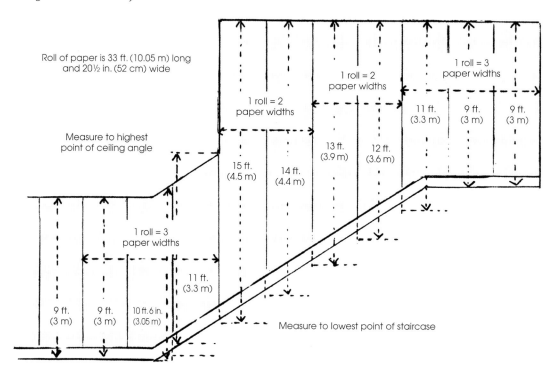

Roll of paper is 33 ft. (10.05 m) long and 20½ in. (52 cm) wide

Measure to highest point of ceiling angle

1 roll = 3 paper widths

1 roll = 2 paper widths

1 roll = 2 paper widths

1 roll = 3 paper widths

11 ft. (3.3 m) 9 ft. (3 m) 9 ft. (3 m)

13 ft. (3.9 m) 12 ft. (3.6 m)

15 ft. (4.5 m) 14 ft. (4.4 m)

1 roll = 3 paper widths

11 ft. (3.3 m)

9 ft. (3 m) 9 ft. (3 m) 10 ft. 6 in. (3.05 m)

Measure to lowest point of staircase

DECORATOR'S DODGE

If the walls of the room are to be decorated, it is easier to mark off the ceiling widths on the upper wall area. Do this on a straight section of wall, rather than on the fireplace wall.

Height of walls from skirting to ceiling	7 ft.–7 ft. 6 in. (2.15–2.30 m)	7 ft. 6 in.–8 ft. (2.30–2.45 m)	8 ft.–8 ft. 6 in. (2.45–2.60 m)	8 ft. 6 in.–9 ft. (2.60–2.75 m)	9 ft.–9 ft. 6 in. (2.75–2.90 m)	9 ft. 6 in.–10 ft. (2.90–3.05 m)	10 ft.–10 ft. 6 in. (3.05–3.20 m)
30 ft. (9 m)	4	5	5	5	6	6	6
34 ft. (10 m)	5	5	5	5	6	6	7
38 ft. (12 m)	5	6	6	6	7	7	8
42 ft. (13 m)	6	6	7	7	7	8	8
46 ft. (14 m)	6	7	7	7	8	8	9
50 ft. (15 m)	7	7	8	8	9	9	10
54 ft. (16 m)	7	8	9	9	9	10	10
58 ft. (17 m)	8	8	9	9	10	10	11
62 ft. (18 m)	8	9	10	10	10	11	12
66 ft. (19 m)	9	9	10	10	11	12	13
67 ft. (20 m)	9	9	10	11	11	12	13
70 ft. (21 m)	9	10	11	11	12	12	13
74 ft. (22 m)	10	10	12	12	12	13	14
78 ft. (23 m)	10	11	12	12	13	14	15
80 ft. (24 m)	11	11	13	13	14	14	16
83 ft. (25 m)	11	11	13	13	14	14	16
86 ft. (26 m)	12	12	14	14	14	15	16
90 ft. (27 m)	12	13	14	14	15	16	17
94 ft. (28 m)	13	13	15	15	15	16	18
98 ft. (30 m)	13	14	15	15	16	17	19

Note: The measurements and the quantity of rolls are approximate.

Types of Paste and Their Applications

Just as there are numerous types of wallpaper, there are also a number of paste products to match.

Cellulose-Based Pastes

Supplied in packets, this product comes in a granular powder, which can be sprinkled into cold water and stirred until it forms a gel-like paste. The advantage of this type is that it is easy to mix and will not go off (spoil) when kept for short periods. Some contain a fungicide, which is useful to protect paper from mold growth. This type is supplied as general purpose or all purpose and can be mixed to various strengths (follow manufacturer's instructions). It can also be mixed to a size-coating consistency. Use for hanging lining paper, woodchip, washable paper, vinyl, blown vinyl, and most types of normal wallpaper.

Ready-Mixed, Extra-Strong, All-Purpose Adhesive

Supplied ready to use in tubs in a white paste-like consistency, it is used for paper-backed and fabric-backed heavyweight vinyl and textured vinyl. A small quantity of the paste can be diluted to use as a size coat.

Border and Overlap Adhesive

Very strong ready-mixed adhesive supplied in small tubs and tubes, this paste is suitable for sticking borders over vinyl surfaces, and used for overlapping seams. Also useful when sticking paper, such as borders, to painted surfaces.

Dextrin-Based Adhesives

Dextrin is derived from starch. The adhesive, supplied as a powder in packets, is mixed first by sprinkling the powder into warm water to form a batter-like consistency, then by pouring in boiling water while stirring vigorously, until the mixture turns (becomes thick). The mixed paste has to be allowed to cool before using. It is a good idea to gently run cold water down the stirring stick so that a layer of water covers the surface and prevents the paste from skinning. Later when cold, the paste can be diluted with cold water and mixed to the working consistency required. There is also a cold-water mixing variety available.

Note: When using dextrin/starch-based adhesives, it is necessary to use glue size, supplied as brown granules in packets, which is mixed with boiling water and allowed to cool before use.

Pasting Methods

1. Always arrange the paste table across a light source, so that it is easy to see by the shine of the paste if the paper is completely covered.
2. If you do not have a paste table, it is possible to use a flush door resting on four chairs.
3. Tie a length of string or wire between the handles of the paste bucket so that it is possible to rest the paste brush on top.

DECORATOR'S DODGE
Keep a bucket of warm water and a sponge below the paste table to use for keeping the edges of the paste table clean.

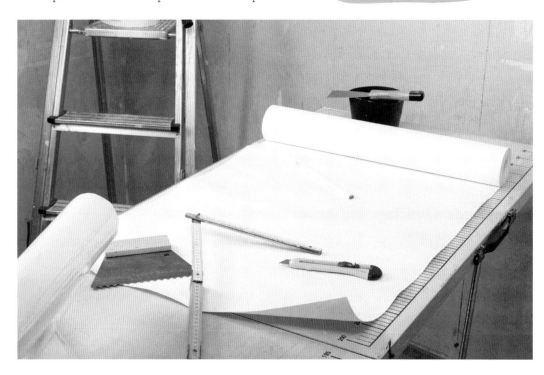

Applying Paste

Always paste from the middle of the length of paper towards the edges of the paper. Apply first toward the far edge (Diagram 1) then pull the paper toward the near edge of the table and paste toward the nearside edge (Diagram 2). Never brush toward the paper edge (Diagram 3), as this will force paste to the underside of the paper, and could mark the face of the paper.

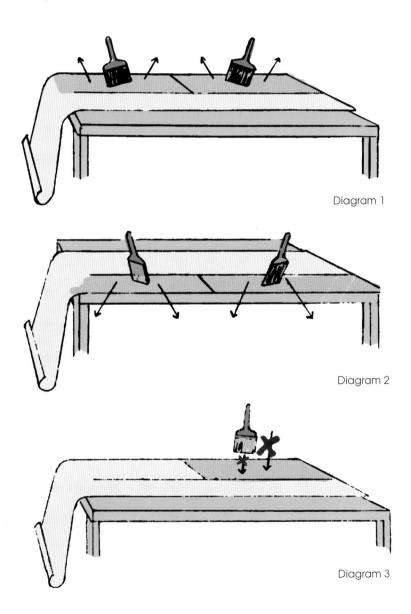

Diagram 1

Diagram 2

Diagram 3

Folding the paper when pasting

Having pasted the first part of the length, in the case of room-sized lengths, you fold the pasted paper back over upon itself (Diagram 1).

In the case of longer lengths for high rooms or staircase walls, the paper is folded "concertina" fashion (pasted side to pasted side). Each table-length is pasted, with the folds being a size that allows the remaining paper on the table to be pasted (Diagram 2).

Having continued pasting to the end of the length, the last section is folded over onto itself (Diagram 3).

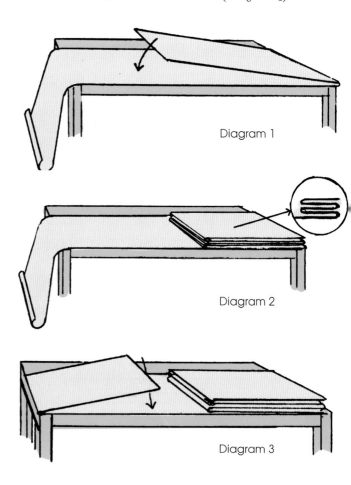

Diagram 1

Diagram 2

Diagram 3

Applying Paste with a Roller

Mix the paste to a slightly thicker consistency than recommended by the adhesive's instructions, then apply the paste with a short pile roller. It is quicker than brushing and applies an even coat of paste. This is also a good method when using ready-mixed tub paste (which is quite thick).

Roll in direction of arrows in a one-way direction at four sections of the paper. One paste-loaded roller usually applies enough for one of the four sections. Roll outward away from the edges of the paper, not in toward the paper edges, to avoid paste creeping underneath the edges and onto the face of the paper.

Note: Only pull the roller in one direction, not backward and forward in the usual fashion as this can cause lumps in the paper.

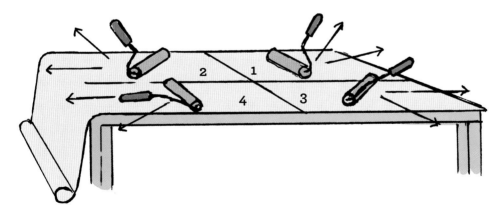

A similar technique to the above can be used when pasting wide borders, using a 2–3 in. (5–7.5 cm) wide short pile roller and thick border adhesive.

1. Roll one way only, toward the end of a length of border and outward toward the far edge of the border.
2. Roll one way only toward the end of the length of border and outward over the near edge of the border.
3. Concertina-fold the pasted border and continue to roll paste in one direction only, and outward toward the edges of the border, as above.

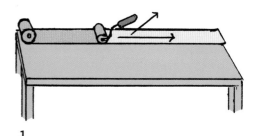

1

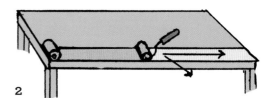

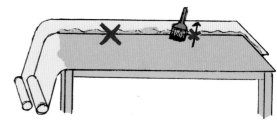

2

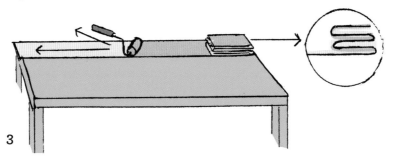

3

Note: It is not a good idea to paste one length of paper on top of another length overlapping the first length, as the length below gets a certain extra amount of paste on it which causes uneven soakage and warping of the length of paper.

Essential Paper-Hanging Tools

Paper-hanging scissors, long-bladed

Small sharp scissors

Paper-hanging brush

Craft knife

Plumb bob

Snap line, chalk, and drawing pins

Wooden folding ruler

Two pencils

Seam roller

Screwdriver

Pasting brush

Sponge

Bucket for paste

Bucket for water

Stirring stick

Other Paper-Hanging Tools and Equipment

- Paste table, stepladder (two stepladders and a plank for ceilings)
- Measuring jug
- Retractable metal measuring tape (needed when estimating long drop walls on staircases)
- Paper-hanging apron with deep pocket (used for tools and essential when papering ceilings)
- Level, for checking horizontal positions
- Small flat-head screwdriver, useful when undoing light switches
- Phillips-head screwdriver
- Medium-pile roller and tray (for applying thick paste)
- And, of course, wallpaper and paste

Hanging Lining Paper

The Purpose of Lining

- To provide a surface that offers a sound adhesion for wallpapers, particularly on nonporous surfaces such as gloss paint (after it has been flatted down) or where a sealer coat has been applied
- To help cover minor surface defects and irregularities, although these should be thoroughly prepared prior to lining
- To provide a surface that can be painted or papered

Hanging Lining Paper to Walls That Will Be Wallpapered

Lengths of lining paper are usually hung horizontally on walls when hung beneath wallpaper so that the joints run horizontally and in the opposite direction to the joints of the subsequent wallpaper.

Pasting and Folding

Because the lengths of lining paper are hung horizontally, some lengths are quite long, and require concertina folding, as shown on page 150.

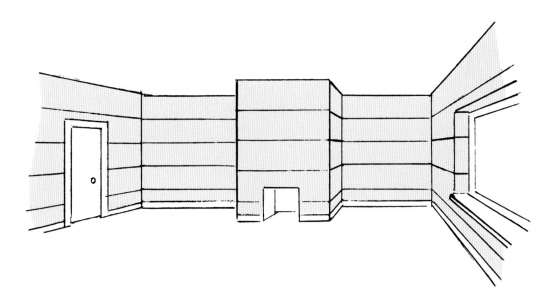

Hanging Technique for Horizontal Lining Paper

1. Paste and concertina-fold the length of paper.

2. Holding the top of the folds with your left hand, place the end of the length near the ceiling line with your right hand. **Note:** The position at this stage does not need to be exact.

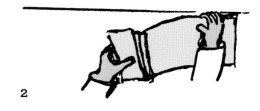

3. Lightly brush the beginning of the length into position, with the paper just turning the wall corner. **Note:** Again, the paper does not need to be in the exact position at this stage.

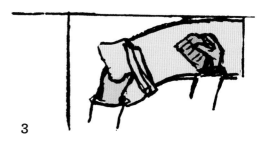

4. Allow one concertina fold to undo, and if the paper is not running parallel to the ceiling, allow a small fold (A) to form in the paper, then maneuver the width of paper up and down (B) until it is running parallel with the ceiling, (just below the ceiling). Then, brush along the wall letting go of one fold at a time (C). Brush down the center of the length and outward toward the edges of the paper, as you move along the wall to the other end of the wall.

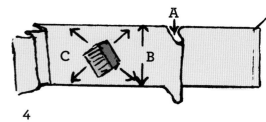

5. Pull back the paper from the first partly stuck end. Pull back enough to be able to remove the small fold.

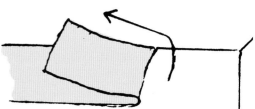

6. Lightly brush down the pulled-back paper and gently tap it so that the paper wraps around the corner slightly.

7. Mark a pencil line down the corner.

8. Pull back the paper slightly and cut along the pencil line.

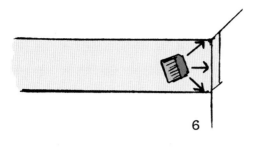

6

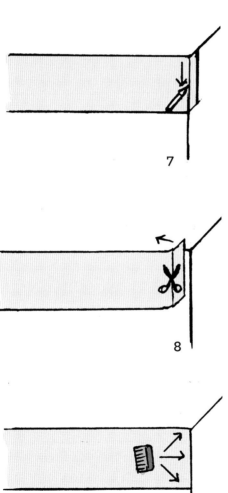

7

8

9

9. Brush the paper back down into place and repeat steps 5 to 8 at the other end of the paper.
10. Hang the remaining lengths below, leaving a slight gap between the joints.
11. When you get close to the bottom of the wall, you will usually need a part- width of paper or a narrow strip to complete hanging the wall.

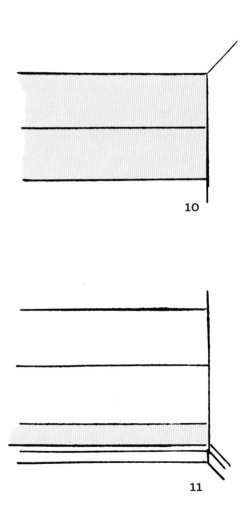

10

11

Marking and Cutting

You can create a narrow width of paper as follows:

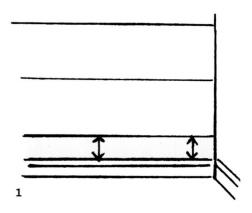

1. Measure the depth of the wall, from the last full width of paper to the baseboard. Do this at more than one place along the wall; the width may vary.

2. Hold a rule at the edge of the paste table, at the measured paper width distance. Place a finger down the side of the paste table to form a guide. Hold a pencil at the far end of the ruler. Move the ruler and the guiding finger down the table edge, keep the pencil pressed onto the paper (this results in a straight pencil mark down the length of paper). Cut the marked length of paper into two pieces.

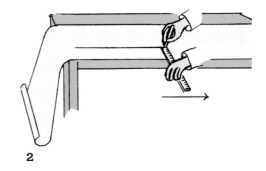

It is a good idea to mark both pieces of paper with arrows (in pencil) pointing to the two original outside straight edges (not the cut edges). This will make sure that you use the uncut edges when hanging the strip up to the previously hung length above.

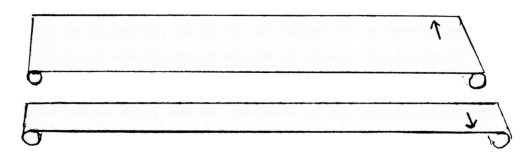

Note: After hanging the measured strip, keep the other cut length, as it will come in handy for the bottom of another wall, or other narrow areas. It may be necessary to measure, mark, and recut the strip.

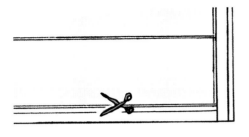

Trimming

Where trimming is necessary at doors, windows, baseboards, and light switches it is best to cut the paper away slightly from these areas, then no lining paper will show behind the wallpaper.

Joints

Never try to butt-joint lining paper, as any slight lap can show up when it is papered over. It is best to aim for a slight gap between the lengths.

Lining Narrow Wall Areas

Sometimes to avoid joints and for ease of application, narrow areas can be lined vertically. If it takes more than one width of paper, try to work it so that the vertical joints will be at a different position to where the wallpaper joint will be.

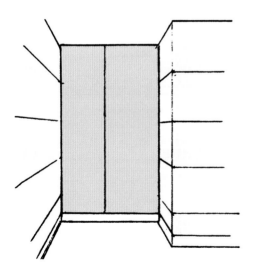

Sometimes for convenience you can paste a length of paper, leaving one end unpasted. This end is left folded back unstuck to the surface. When the length has thoroughly dried out, the folded flap can be torn off across itself, leaving a "feathered" off area.

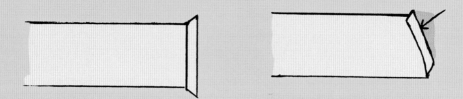

This tear-off flap method would be useful on a narrow piece of wall, for example at the side of a large window. The tear-off dry flap is near the horizontal joint of length above window, where the arrow is pointing.

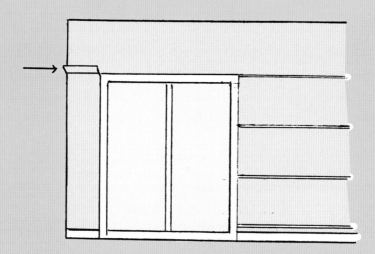

Hanging Lining Paper on Walls to Be Painted

For hanging technique, see Hanging Wallpaper on Walls, page 179. The lining paper is hung vertically, as this creates less joints at eye level than when hung horizontally (1). Each length should be hung with very slight gaps between lengths and not overlapped (2). The slight gaps between lengths should be small enough to flood and fill when paint is applied to the surface (3).

Should the gaps between the lengths prove too wide to flood with paint, these can be surface-filled with a fine powder filler and lightly sanded when dry, prior to painting.

After lining and before painting, any imperfections in the walls that show through the lining paper can be carefully filled and sanded.

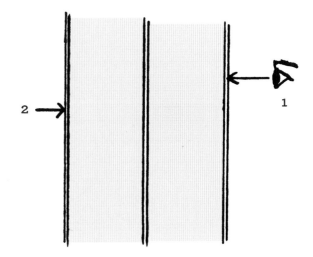

Hanging Lining Paper to Ceilings

For the actual hanging technique, see Hanging Ceiling Paper, opposite page. Lining paper is usually hung with the length of the room, which is the opposite direction to the wallpaper that follows (which is hung across the width of the room). This is so the joints of the two papers do not run in the same direction, which avoids joints occurring in the same position.

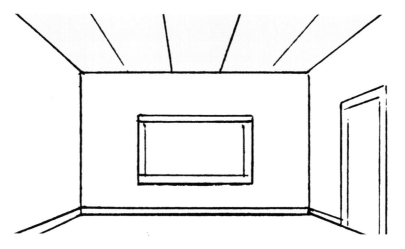

Alternatively, sometimes the lining paper is hung in the same direction as the wallpaper, but positioned at a different starting point, so that the joints do not occur in the same position. To do this, the first length of lining paper is hung as a part-width from the starting point.

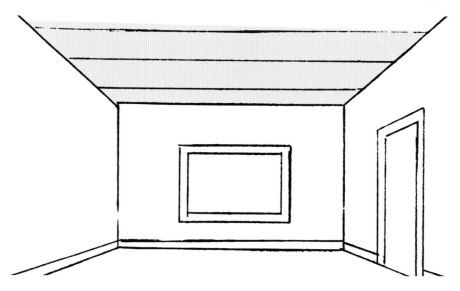

Hanging Ceiling Paper

It is usual with most ceilings to hang lengths of paper across the main light source, usually a window. This means that as you look across the ceiling, only a small section of the joint is illuminated to the eyes.

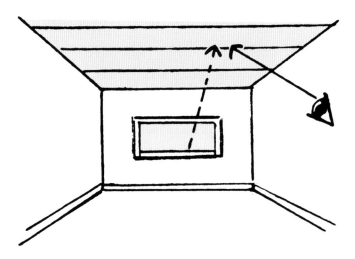

If the paper is hung in the same direction as the light source, more of the joints are illuminated to the eyes.

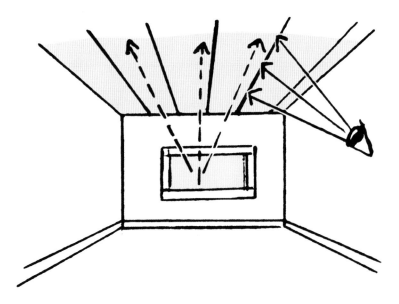

Exceptions to the Hanging Ceiling Paper Rule

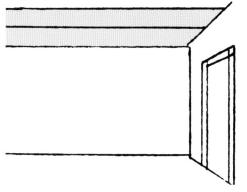

Narrow ceilings, such as some halls and landings

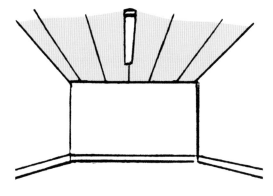

Ceilings where there is an obstacle, such as a strip light

"L"-shaped ceilings

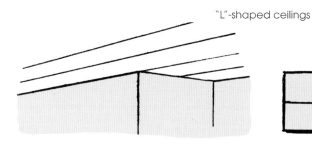

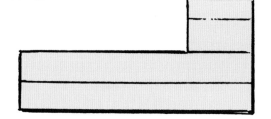

Plan view of ceiling

On Which Side of the Room Should I Start?

Start at the side without obstructions. In this case the side opposite the fireplace wall projection. This makes it easier to follow the paper's pattern.

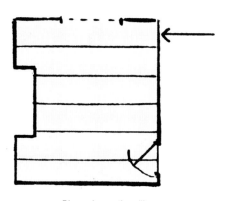

Plan view of ceiling

Paper-Hanging a Ceiling

Necessary Tools and Equipment

- Paste table
- Bucket for mixed paste
- Wide flat brush to apply the paste
- Bucket for rinsing water and a sponge
- Part-roll of paper to use as a support ("jockey") for pasted and folded lengths
- Long length of fine string, to use as a snap line
- Colored chalk (for chalk line). Note: Not red or purple, as they can cause "bleeding"
- Drawing pins, to hold the chalk line
- Two stepladders
- A plank long enough to span the room
- A paper-hangers apron with a deep pocket, essential for keeping tools handy when standing on a ladder or a plank

Hanging Techniques
Measuring and Folding

Measure the first length, usually the width of the room. It is easier to measure the floor. Add 2 in. (5 cm) at either side of the room, to allow for marking and cutting.

Decide what part of the pattern you want at the beginning of the first length (this can be done on the paste table). Remember to leave the extra 2 in. (5 cm) beyond the chosen pattern for marking and cutting. Cut off the surplus.

Measure the length of paper required, by first measuring and marking out the top of the paste table. An average paste table is about 6 ft. (183 cm) long, so it is convenient to make a mark at 5 ft. (152.5 cm) on the table. When measuring, say, 10 ft. (305 cm), you stretch the paper across the board, then fold it back on itself for cutting.

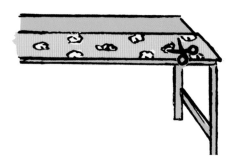

When measuring lesser amounts, stretch the paper along the table, then turn it back on itself and measure the remaining piece with a folding ruler. Cut at the appropriate measurement.

For longer pieces, keep stretching the paper out along the paste table and folding back on itself. Then use the ruler to measure the extra amount beyond the 5 ft. (152.5 cm) sections.

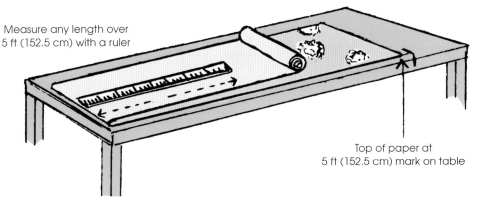

Measure any length over
5 ft (152.5 cm) with a ruler

Top of paper at
5 ft (152.5 cm) mark on table

Matching Patterns

Having cut the first length, it is a good idea to make sure that it is the right length (before cutting any more lengths) by spreading it out across a clean section of floor, between the two sidewalls. Having been checked, further lengths can be pattern-matched on the paste table and cut.

Lay out the first length along the table so that it hangs partly over long edge of the table (A); this leaves a spare width of table top on which the second roll of paper can be laid out (B).

Next move the roll of laid-out paper up and down the length of the table until a pattern alignment occurs with the first length.

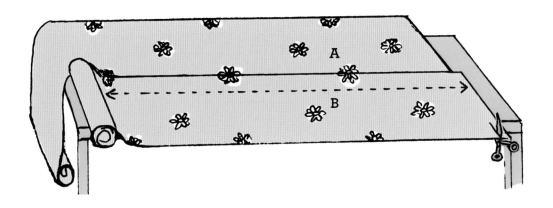

Rolling Up and Cutting

After getting a match, cut off the spare paper at the top of the second length then place the second roll on top of the first length and roll up together from the top.

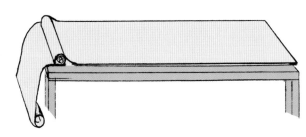

Continue to roll up together, and as you do so, pull the two lengths of paper together toward the top of the board. When you get to the end of the first length, place a heavy object such as a paper-hanging brush on top of the paper, to stop it moving about.

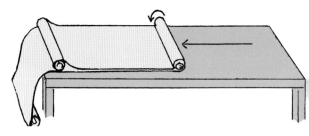

Take the top roll out beyond the bottom end of the first length, and cut off to the same length as the first length. Remember to allow extra for measuring and cutting. Continue the above steps with the other rolls to create more lengths.

Notes:

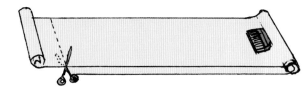

- It is a good idea not to cut too many lengths at once, in case of mistakes and because some lengths may have to be shorter at places, for example over fireplaces.
- With an alternating pattern, it is best to work from two rolls to save paper (see wallpaper patterns, page 128).

Having cut the lengths, roll them up and place them on a clean drop cloth, leaving the first length of paper on the table on its own ready for pasting. With an indefinite pattern, it is a good idea to mark the back of each length with a "T" (for top).

Preparing a Starting Point on the Ceiling

Because the corners where ceilings and walls meet are very rarely straight, it is not a good idea to hang the first length of paper into one of these corners. It is essential that the first length is hung in a straight line, and not swung sideways, otherwise all the following lengths will also have to be swung sideways to correspond. It is usual to hang from a straight line; to achieve this, complete the following steps.

1. Measure just less than the width of a roll of paper (about ½ in. or 12 mm less).

2. Place two stepladders and a plank at the starting point, and mark out the measurement at both sides of the ceiling where you are intending to start. Ideally, the plank should be at a height that brings your eye level close to the ceiling. Apply colored chalk to a long length of fine string (do not use red or purple which can "bleed").

3. Using heavy-duty drawing pins, attach the chalked string so that it stretches out across the ceiling (across the measured marks).

4. Gently pull the string downward, then let it go so that it snaps back to the ceiling. This should leave a straight line of chalk.

5. This is the straight line to which the edge of the first length of paper is placed.

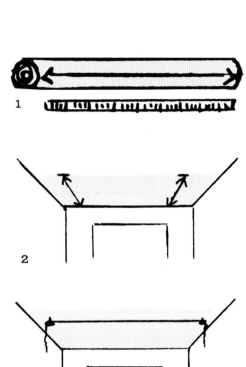

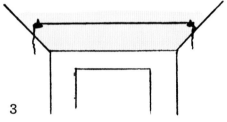

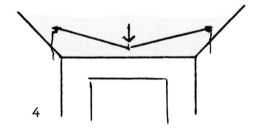

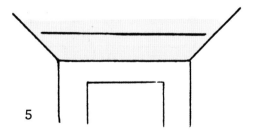

Pasting and Folding

The paper is pasted and folded in concertina folds (see page 170).

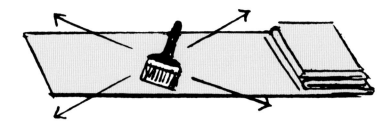

Supporting the Pasted Paper

The concertina-pasted and folded paper is placed onto a part roll of wallpaper to act as a support. The part roll is sometimes called a "jockey."

Placing and Hanging Ceiling Paper

Until you get the hang of it (literally) it is not a bad idea to get someone else to hold the "jockey" and supported paper.

1. Undo the first concertina fold and place the beginning of the length of paper at the starting point on the ceiling so that the paper turns around slightly onto the wall. Try to get the edge of the paper running along the snapped chalk line. Keep the "jockey" support up toward the ceiling, and move it slightly to the right or left to maneuver and steer the paper along the line.

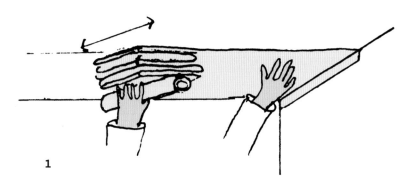

1

2. Don't worry at this stage if the beginning of the paper is not in the exact position, because you can allow a small fold to form (A) then hang from there. As you let each concertina unfold, one at a time, continue to steer the paper along the snapped line by moving the "jockey" support slightly to right or left, and brushing the paper onto the ceiling from the center outward. **Note:** Remember to keep the "jockey" roll as near to the ceiling as possible as this makes it easier to steer the length. There is less chance of tearing the paper by putting the paper-hanging brush through it and less chance of further concertina folds dropping out before you are ready.

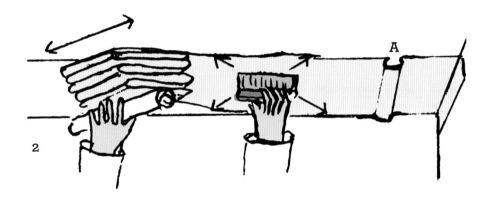

3. Continue undoing concertina folds and steering the paper by moving the "jockey" to right or left, and brushing the paper onto the ceiling until you arrive at the other end of the ceiling (B). Then brush and tap the paper so that it laps down onto the wall.

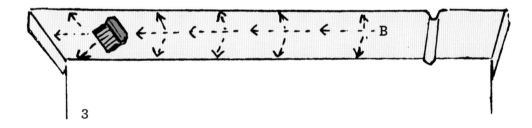

Scoring and Cutting

1. Drag the back of the points of the scissors into the ceiling/wall corner angle; this will produce a "scored" line. Sometimes a scored line is not clearly visible; if so, use a pencil to make a line just below the corner.
2. If you place a finger between the pencil and the corner, it acts as a guide for the pencil line.
3. Pull back the scored paper off the ceiling. Support the paper with one hand and cut along the scored line with the other.
4. Wipe off any surplus paste on the wall with a damp sponge, then brush down the section.
5. Return to the starting point and pull off the paper to a point beyond the small fold. Place the "jockey" below the loose paper, then brush the paper back onto the ceiling. Remove any surplus paste from the wall. Mark and cut, as at the other end of the paper.

Hanging the Remaining Lengths

This is done in the same way as the first length, except that the beginning of the length is placed lightly on the ceiling, after first getting the pattern to line up with the corresponding pattern at the edge of the first length.

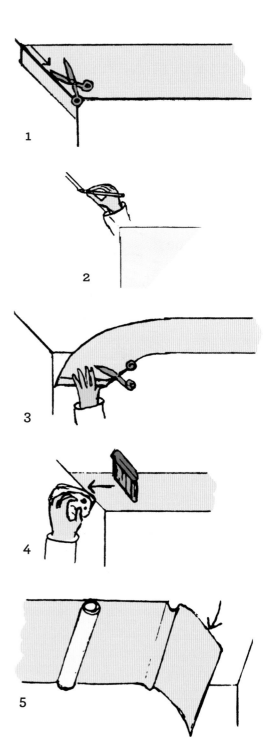

This is done by moving the paper backward and forward (A). The best way is to roughly line up the pattern as you place the paper, then gently slide the paper into position and, at the same time, check that the edge of the paper will form a good butt joint (not a lap joint). If the paper pattern is way out of line—or if the second length is not going to run in line with the first and not forming a good joint—pull the paper off and, if necessary, re-paste the beginning. Next, reposition the start of the length. This is better than trying to shove the paper around with a papering brush. When the pattern is aligned and the edge of the paper is running in line with the edge of the first length, carry on letting out concertina folds, one at a time, and brushing the paper along the middle and out toward the edges.

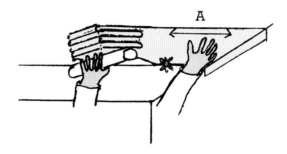

Seam Rolling

The purpose of seam rolling is to secure the paper to the ceiling. Some joints have a bad habit of curling off slightly when the paper is first placed on the ceiling. When joints (or seams) are rolled during hanging, care has to be taken to avoid crushing the pattern of some textured papers. Also, care must be taken not to cause polishing to delicate flat-matte papers.

Paper Joints

With most paper it is usual to butt joint (where the papers just meet), but there are exceptions where leaving a slight gap between lengths is necessary:

- **When hanging lining paper that is to receive wallpaper or be painted**
- **When hanging woodchip that is to be painted**
- **When hanging anaglypta or embossed papers that are to be painted**

The gap is left in all these instances so that when the joints are flooded with paint, they do not show as much.

Papering around a Hanging Light Fixture

Before hanging and trimming pasted paper near electric fixtures, it is vitally important to turn off the power at source to avoid electrocution. Then, remove the lampshade and the bulb to reduce the size of the obstruction.

1. Brush the length of paper up to the center of the light fixture (A) and keep the paper supported on the "jockey" held close to the ceiling. Make a hole in the paper with the points of the scissors, near the center of the light fixture. Then, make a cut from the center of the hole outward toward the edge of the light fixture (B).

2. Next, make two more cuts from the center hole toward the sides of the light fixture, and then two more cuts in between the first three cuts. Gently lower the end of the light and flex through the cut.

3. Then, make three further cuts from the center hole to the far edges of the light fixture to form a star shape. **Note:** When making these cuts, it is a good idea to first make short cuts, then press the paper against the light fixture to feel the shape. Then extend the cuts to the edge of the light fixture.

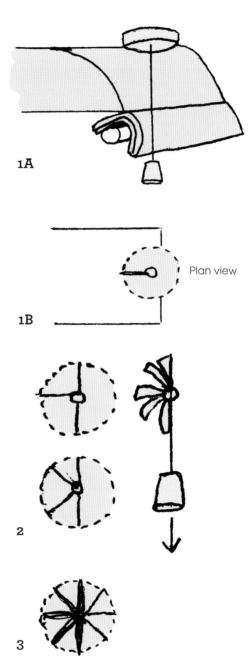

1A

1B

Plan view

2

3

4. Carry on at this stage with hanging the remainder of the length of paper. Then when hung and trimmed to the walls, come back to the light fixture and deal with the paper as follows. Mark the back of the star-shaped cut flaps with a pencil, where they are in contact with the ceiling fixture.

5. If the ceiling fixture is in a fixed location, cut off the flaps slightly to the outside of the pencil marks using small scissors. Or, trim off the flaps with a sharp knife if the paper will allow it without tearing.

If the ceiling fixture will unscrew, remove the outside part of the fixture. Brush the star-cut paper flaps around the fixed part of the fixture, mark, and cut slightly to outside of the pencil marks. Next, smooth the paper down around the fitting and pull up and screw on the outside of the fitting. Wipe off any surplus paste on the light fixture with a damp sponge, making sure that the power is still off. **Safety note:** Make sure the electricity supply has been cut off at source before following these instructions. Great care should be taken with this method not to inadvertently cut through any fine electric wires.

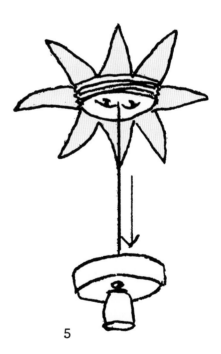

Alternative Method

First make sure that the power supply to the light is still turned off. Remove the bulb and the lampshade. Again, great care should be taken not to inadvertently cut through any fine electric wires.

1. Brush the paper right up to the ceiling light, hold over it, and feel for the center of the fitting through the paper.
2. Make a hole, followed by a cut from the hole, toward the edge of the light fixture. This should be the nearest edge toward you.
3. Press the paper up to the light fixture and feel for the edges of the light fixture. Make further cuts from the center hole toward these edges (A), and press the paper down over the fixture, so that the paper flaps stick outward (B).
4. Make further cuts from the center hole toward the far side of the fixture until a star shape is formed.
5. Mark where the top of the cut flaps touches the light fixture with a pencil. Next, cut along the pencil lines with either small scissors or sharp bladed knife. Wipe any surplus paste off the light fixture and tap down the paper into place with a paper-hanging brush.

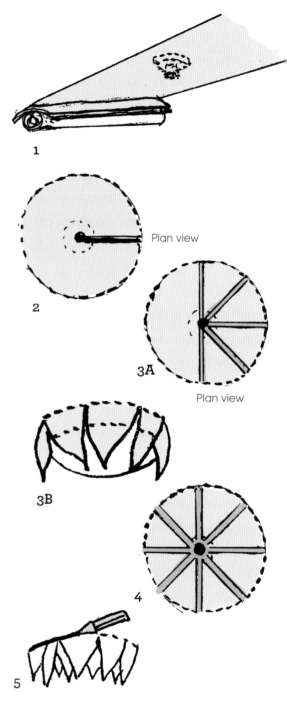

1

2

Plan view

3A

Plan view

3B

4

5

Papering around a Round (Ceiling-Fixed) Pull Cord Switch

Use the same techniques as above, except pass the pull cord through the star-shaped cut.
Note: If the cord does not undo from the fitting, the cord can be shortened by tying it to itself (making less cord to pass through the star cut).

Papering around a Square Obstruction (Such as a Pull Cord Switch)

1. Take the pasted paper above and slightly beyond the square fixture. Feel the shape of the fixture through the paper. Make a hole with the scissor points near the center of the fixture. Feel for the corners of the fixture and make four cuts from the center hole out toward the corners.

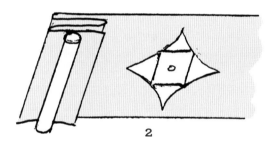

1

2. Turn back the four paper flaps that cutting to the corners has produced.

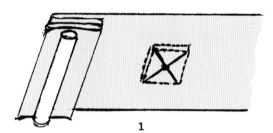

2

3. Press down the paper and the flaps surrounding the square obstruction. Hang the remaining length of paper, then come back and cut off the flaps with a very sharp knife.

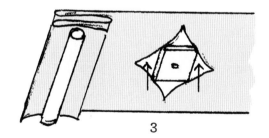

3

Avoiding a Fixture Coming in the Center of a Width of Paper

Because it is quite difficult to cut a star-shape when it is in the center of a width of paper, you may prefer to use another technique that avoids a light fixture coming in the center and instead comes at the edge of the paper. To do this, follow these instructions:

1. Measure back from the center of the light fixture in paper widths toward the paper-hanging starting point (usually near the window wall).

2. Mark out these paper widths on the ceiling until you come to the last mark near the wall, which is usually closer to the wall than a paper width. Measure this width.

3. Measure and mark a pencil line on the back of the paper (using the techniques explained on page 158). **Note:** Make sure that you are marking from the correct edge of the paper. Cut the marked paper.

4. Hang the cut narrow width of paper to a snapped chalk line (see page 169).

5. The light fixture is at paper joint position, which means that you only have to do a half-star cut from the edges of the paper.

Note: Where there are two fixtures, the above technique will work for the first one, but unless you are very lucky, it will not bring the paper joint to the middle of the second fixture.

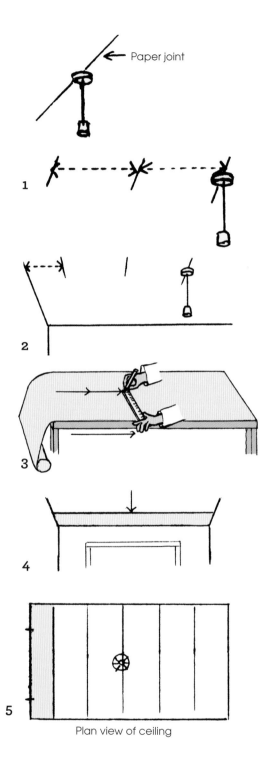

Paper joint

Plan view of ceiling

Hanging Wallpaper on Walls

The necessary requirements when hanging wallpaper are much the same as the ones listed for ceilings except that one stepladder is sufficient. Before papering a room, use a roll of wallpaper as a measuring aid, and mark off in pencil or chalk from a decided starting point in the room (A) in order to see how the joints will work out. Try to work it so that paper joints do not occur at external corners. If this occurs, change the starting point or hang less than a full width of paper at the starting point.

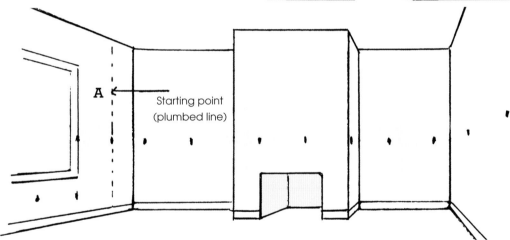

A ← Starting point
(plumbed line)

The usual starting point is from the side of the window or the internal corner of a window wall. Starting from the window means you will be hanging from the main light source, and consequently, the joints will not show as much.

DECORATOR'S DODGE

If the room you are decorating is already papered, note where the starting point and joints are before stripping the wallpaper off. This will give you some idea where to start.

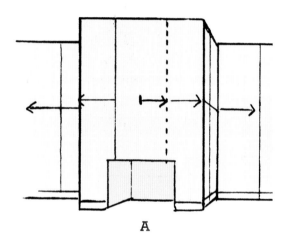

A

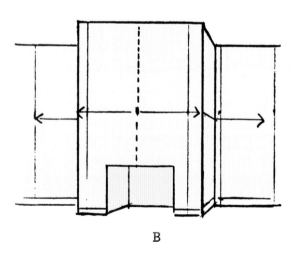

B

Hanging on a Center Point on a Fireplace or Feature Wall

Sometimes when wallpaper has a definite, bold and regular pattern, it may be best to work from the center of the fireplace or feature wall and hang from each side of the center around the room. Depending on how the pattern and the joints work out, the paper is hung either side of a vertical centerline (A) OR over the center by marking out half a width of paper distance from the center of the wall and hanging from there (B). The vertical line should be straight.

Hanging Vertically Straight

Whatever starting point you choose, it is essential to hang to a vertically plumbed line. This is especially important when you hang around internal and external corners (see page 182).

1. Measure a width of paper distance from the starting point, usually the window, and make a small mark toward the top of the wall.

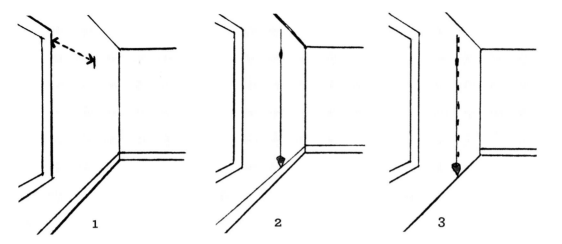

2. Next, hold the plumb bob line (or weight on fine string) to the mark on the wall, and allow the weight to swing freely before coming to a stop.

3. While holding the plumb bob to the mark, make a series of vertical marks alongside the string down the wall (care being taken not to move the string). These are the marks to which you hang the edge of the paper. Getting your first length vertically plumb will mean you avoid having to swing subsequent lengths of paper across, providing you keep each length vertical.

Measuring

Measure the height of the room, then measure the first length on the paste table. Remember to allow an extra 2 in. (5 cm) at the top and the bottom of the length for marking and cutting. It is not a bad idea, having measured and cut the first length, to hold it up to the wall (before it is pasted) to check the length. Line up the pattern as described in matching patterns pages 127 and 167. Next, measure and cut subsequent lengths of paper (not too many in case of mistakes), then roll up the lengths and place on a clean drop cloth. This avoids pasting overlapping lengths on the paste table, which can cause uneven soakage.

DECORATOR'S DODGE

- When the lengths are cut, it is a good idea to mark the back of the paper at the beginning of the length, with a "T" (for top). With indefinite patterns, this avoids hanging the paper upside down.

- When using craft knives with loose blades, it is a good idea to mark in pencil each end of the blade with numbers 1 and 2 or a cross at one end so that you know which end of the blade has been used.

Internal Corners

Check with a plumb bob when cutting
and hanging at an internal corner.

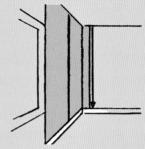

External Corners

Check with a plumb line when turning paper around external corners, as you
would find on fireplace walls (A). It is a good idea to check for plumb when
hanging around obstacles, such as doorways, where in addition to checking the
length that comes beyond the door, it is necessary to check the short lengths
above the door (B).

This also applies to windows, where it is advisable to check for plumb above and
below the window, as well as at the side of the window (C).

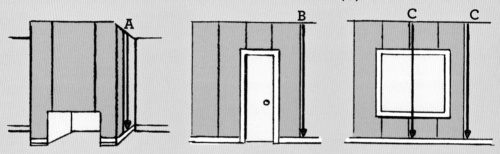

Deciding Where Paper Will Meet Up

When you have papered around a room, there has to be a finishing point where
the paper meets up. This meeting point is best if it is on a short piece of wall (A),
or where it will be out of sight, such as near a window, where curtains will conceal
most of it (B), or in an internal corner hidden by a projecting external corner (C).

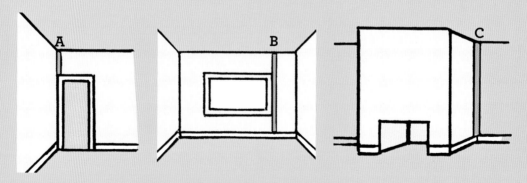

Paper-Hanging Techniques

Pasting and Folding

Unless the lengths of paper are for a taller-than-average room, there will be no need to use concertina folds. When pasting, one fold at the top of the board and one fold at the bottom will be sufficient.

With slightly longer lengths it is only necessary to fold the top twice and the bottom of the length once.

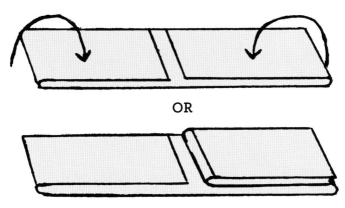

OR

Handling and Positioning the Paper

1. Following pasting, make a small ½ in. (13 mm) fold along the top edge of the paper (A). This creates a dry area of paper to hold. It also means that a strip of dry paper will touch the ceiling. Next, holding the dry fold, lift up and undo the pasted fold at the top of the length (B).

2. Pick up the length of paper (C). Leave the bottom fold in place at this stage. Carry the length of paper over to the starting point on the wall—to where the vertical plumb line marks are—and place the top of the length near the ceiling and the edge of the paper near the vertically plumbed marks.

3. Before brushing the paper onto the wall, first make sure that the edge of the paper is running parallel with the vertically plumbed marks. To do this, maneuver the paper into position by lifting or lowering the top of the paper slightly at the side of the paper furthest away from the plumbed marks.

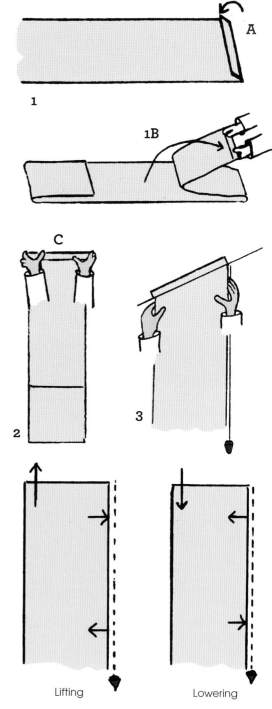

Lifting The left-hand top edge causes the top of the paper to swing toward the plumbed line and the bottom of the paper to swing away from the plumbed line.

Lowering The left-hand top edge causes the top of the paper to swing away from the plumbed line and the bottom of the paper to swing toward the plumbed line.

4. Having placed the paper in line with the plumbed marks, lightly brush the top of the length onto the top of the wall, brushing up and down the middle of the length and out toward the edges of the paper. **Note:** If you find that the length is not running vertically parallel to the plumbed marks, peel the paper off the wall and start again. This is preferable to trying to shove and swing the paper about with the paper-hanging brush, which can result in either stretching the paper or tearing it, or causing wrinkles.

5. When you are sure that the paper is hanging correctly, brush down the center of the length and outward, until you are nearly at the bottom fold. Open up the fold and brush the paper down onto the top of the baseboard. Using the paper-hanging brush, tap the paper lightly into the angle where the baseboard meets the wall.

6. Using the back of the scissor points, score a line along the angle. If the scored line does not show, use a lead pencil along the score. Pull off the bottom of the paper slightly, and cut slightly to the lower side of the line.

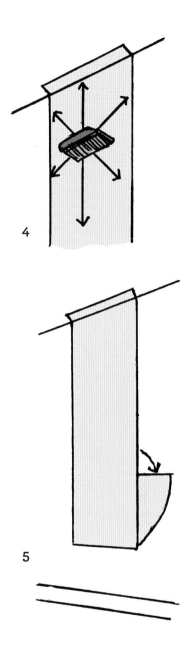

7. Wipe any surplus paste off the baseboard with a damp sponge, then brush the bottom of the paper into place. Return to the top of the length, and using the back of the scissor points, score a line. Pull down the paper (if necessary, pull down the small top fold) until the paper hangs down and the scored line on the back of the paper can be seen.

8. Cut along the scored line, keeping just a fraction to the outside of it (the side nearest the top of the paper). **Note:** If the scored line cannot be easily seen at the back of the paper, then hold the loose paper up, and cut along the scored mark at the front of the paper.

9. Wipe any surplus paste off the ceiling with a damp sponge, then brush the paper upward and outward into position.

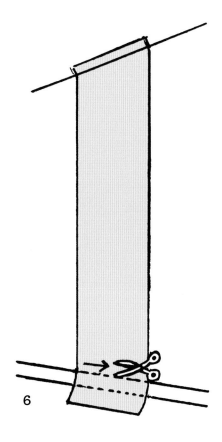

6

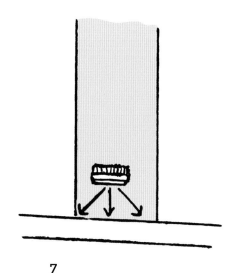

7

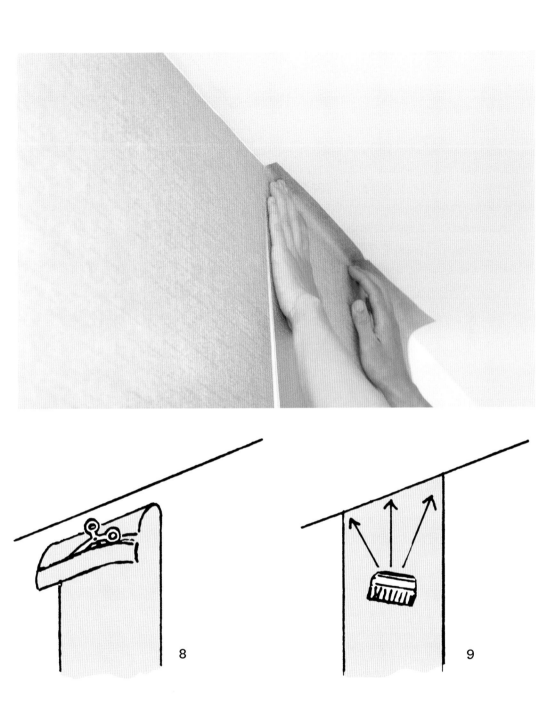

8

9

Papering into and around Internal Corners

1. As you paper toward an internal corner, you will usually find that it will need a part width of paper near the corner. Do not attempt to paper around the corner, as this can cause the length of paper to go out of vertical alignment where it laps around the corner. First measure the distance from the last full width of paper to the corner and add ¼ in. (6 mm) to allow for a small amount of paper to turn around the corner slightly.

2. Next, the width of the section of wall has to be marked out on the width of the paper. This is done by marking, which can be either dry marking, on the back of a dry length of paper, or wet marking, which is done with scissor points on the back of a length of pasted paper.

Dry paper marking Mark a pencil line on the back of the dry paper, following the marking techniques on page 158. **Note:** Make sure that you are marking the correct edge of the paper.

Wet paper marking Paste and fold the top and bottom of the length of paper toward the center of the length, keeping the folded edges of the length exactly parallel with the lower edges of the paper. Then place the lower scissor blade against the end of the wooden measure and the point toward the paper.

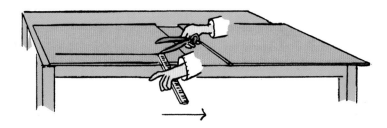

Note: Make sure that you are marking from the correct edge of the paper. Line up the width measured with the edge of the table and keep a finger at the edge of the table to act as a guide. Drag the measure toward you down the length of paper, keeping the scissor point touching the paper and the finger at the measured point at the edge of the table so that the scissor point leaves a slight marked line. Cut down the full length of the marked paper.

Next, turn back the two top folds.

Note: It is a good idea to mark the uncut outside edges with small arrows (on the back of the paper) to avoid confusion as to which is the straight joining edge.

3. Hang the marked and trimmed paper to the first wall, butting to the last length and allowing a small amount of paper to lap on the second wall.

4. Measure the width of this second marked and cut length of paper and mark this width onto the second wall.

5. Hold a plumb line onto the mark then make a series of vertical marks on the wall behind the plumb line. Do not allow the plumb line to swing.

6. Hang the second marked and cut length of paper with the leading edge up to the vertical marks. Score the corner with scissors. Trim off any small amount of paper if necessary, which laps around the internal corner.

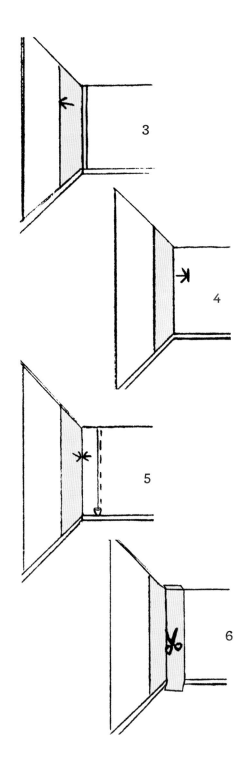

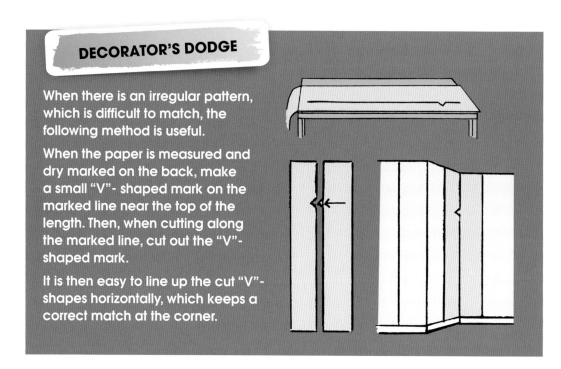

When there is an irregular pattern, which is difficult to match, the following method is useful.

When the paper is measured and dry marked on the back, make a small "V"-shaped mark on the marked line near the top of the length. Then, when cutting along the marked line, cut out the "V"-shaped mark.

It is then easy to line up the cut "V"-shapes horizontally, which keeps a correct match at the corner.

Papering around External Corners

Try to make the wallpaper starting point at a position that causes a wallpaper joint to form just around the external corners, such as fireplace walls and window and door reveal corners. Never position a wallpaper joint right on an external corner, as the paper can easily peel away from the corner.

If you can, try and work it so that there is a narrow "lap round" the corner, then follow these steps. If not, see Hanging an External Corner with a Wide Turnaround of Paper, page 192.

1. Brush the paper onto the face side (usually the widest side) of the wall. Make a cut from the top edge of the paper toward the corner and another cut from the bottom of the paper toward the corner.

2. Gently turn the paper around the corner with your fingers, working from the middle of the length upward toward the ceiling, and downward toward the baseboard. Try to avoid forming wrinkles in the paper. Follow by brushing the paper around the corner in the same upward and downward manner. Trim off the paper flaps at top and bottom of the length.

3. Check the paper turn around for vertical plumb: if it is, then a second length can be hung to the edge; if not, hang a second length to a set of vertically plumbed marks, so that the edge nearest the external corner is just a fraction from the edge.

4. Next, cut down vertically through both layers of paper, using a sharp craft knife against a straight edge or ruler. Lift off the top sheet of wallpaper and peel off the cut strip from the piece underneath.

5. Brush second length down into position so that the two cut edges butt together. Trim off top and bottom paper flaps and brush down the paper. Wipe off any surplus paste on ceiling and baseboard and where the cut edges butt together.

6. Roll the butt joint with a seam roller.

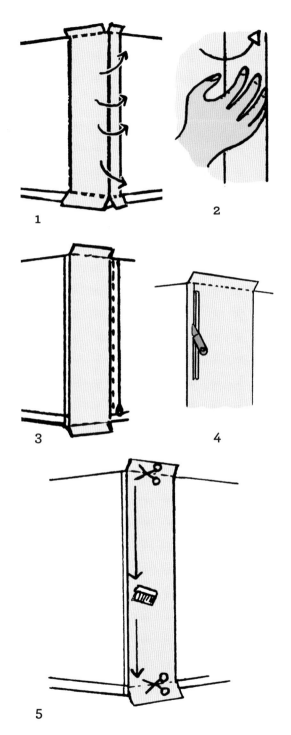

Hanging an External Corner with a Wide Turnaround of Paper

1. Brush the paper onto the face wall and make cuts at the top and bottom of the length, toward the corner. Turn the paper around the corner, as described in step 2 on page 191, brushing from the center toward the top and bottom of the length.

2. Using a sharp-bladed craft knife against a straight edge, cut through the paper a small distance from the corner (1½ in. / 4 cm), right down the length of the paper.

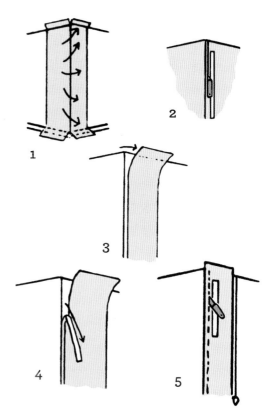

- When hanging a thin, light-colored wallpaper over dark-colored walls, first coat the walls with white or light-colored matte or flat paint, or hang lining paper.

- Always wallpaper in the main light source, the one in which it will be viewed, but check for irregularities such as overlapping joints, with a low-level light, such as a table lamp on a long flex.

- When papering behind or above a door, lock the door or wedge it, to prevent anyone opening the door and causing an accident.

3. Peel the cut length of paper right off the return wall.

4. Reposition the cut length so that it projects outward slightly beyond the corner. Hang to a plumbed line. Using a sharp knife and straight edge, cut through the paper again, this time a fraction from the outside of the corner; remove the cut strip of paper.

5. Turn back the top sheet of paper and peel off the cut strip from the wallpaper underneath. Brush the paper down, cut off the top and bottom flaps of the paper. Remove any surplus paste and roll the butt joint with a seam roller.

Exceptions to the Previous Method

When a length of paper is hung around a corner in a position that produces a wide turnaround of paper (A), then the following may apply.

In certain cases where there is just a short section of wall (such as the side of a fireplace wall) and the paper has an irregular pattern, it is possible to hang into the corner a narrow width of paper (B), which is the cut section of length (C), even if (A) is slightly out of alignment, and lose the variation in the paper width into the corner. Then hang the second part of the cut length to a plumbed line (again losing the variation of paper width into the corner).

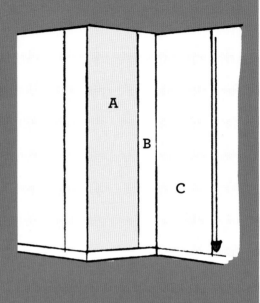

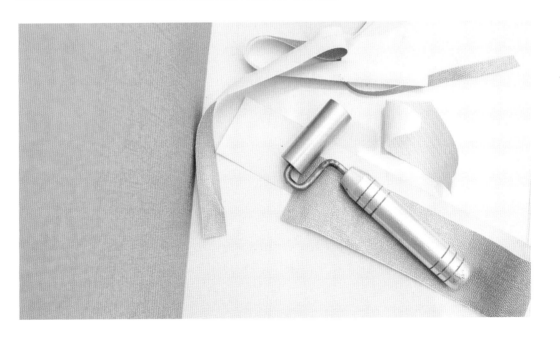

Papering around Obstacles

Papering around Doors

As you paper toward a door, there is nearly always an "L"-shaped piece of wall around the door to deal with.

1. Before pasting the length, measure the width of the paper and add approximately ⅛ in. (2 mm) to the measurement (this allows for paper expansion when soaked with paste). Use a part-roll as a measure and mark the width of the roll from the paper joint above the door onto the wall beyond (A). Hold a vertical plumb line from this mark, and make a series of short vertical lines down the wall at the side of the plumb bob string.

2. Brush only the top of the pasted length onto the wall (B) where it comes down to the doorframe, leaving the lower part of the length and bottom fold hanging off the wall and door. Make the angled corner cut (C).

3. Paste and hang another length matching at the top of the first length (see arrows) and hang to the vertically plumbed marks on the wall. Ignore the bottom of the first length, which is hanging loose at this stage.

4. When the second length is matched to the top of the first and is vertically hung, undo the bottom fold on the first length and hang the remaining paper (shaded on the diagram) to the edge of the second length. Then mark down the doorframe and skirting angles and cut (described earlier). Wipe off surplus paste and brush the paper into position.

5. Sometimes when a short length is needed above a door, it can mean that almost a full width of paper (D) is required, just beyond the door. When this is the case, it is possible to hang the first length and check the leading edge during hanging, with a plumb bob, without first hanging a second length beyond the door (as described above at step 4).

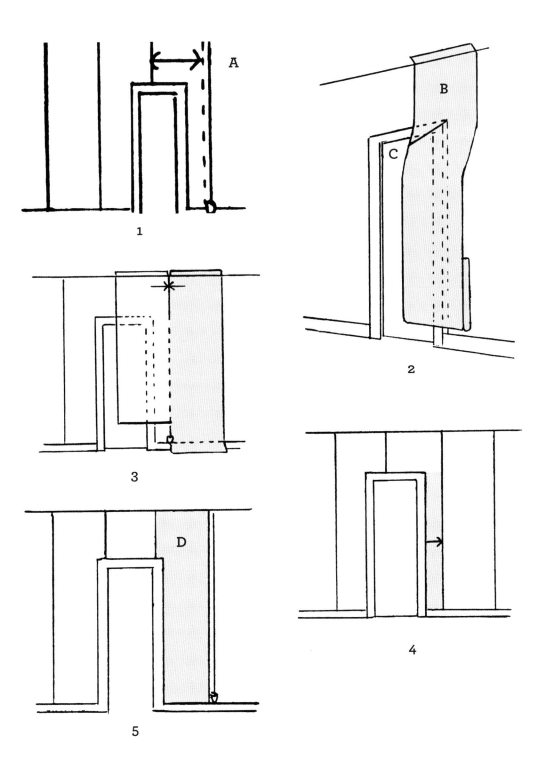

1

2

3

4

5

A

B

C

D

DECORATOR'S DODGE

Before pasting and hanging the paper, hold the cut, dry length up to where it will match the previous length (A). Mark out an area smaller than the door and frame size (shown in the diagram as a dark line), so that the surplus paper (B) can be cut off on the paste table, resulting in less paper to handle and paste.

Place the pasted length above the door and brush onto the wall. Feel for the corner of the doorframe and make a diagonal cut (C) from the edge of the paper, below the doorframe, up to the corner.

This creates two flaps, one above the doorframe, the other down the side of the doorframe. Tap the flaps into the corner angles (where the frame meets the wall) with a paper-hanging brush. Then if the type of paper will allow it, cut down the angles with a sharp-bladed craft knife. Or if the paper is too thin and difficult to cut with a blade, mark the angles with a pencil or the back of a scissor point.

Pull the length of paper up from the bottom of the wall so that it is possible to cut up the marked line with scissors.

Note: To avoid tearing the paper, use a sharp-bladed knife or small pointed scissors for the top of the cut, near the corner of the doorframe (see short dark line at D). When the section of paper has been cut and removed, wipe surplus paste off the edge of the doorframe with a damp sponge, before brushing the length into position.

When you paper beyond the door, it usually requires another "L"-shaped piece of paper. As with the first piece, get rid of surplus paper while the length is dry.

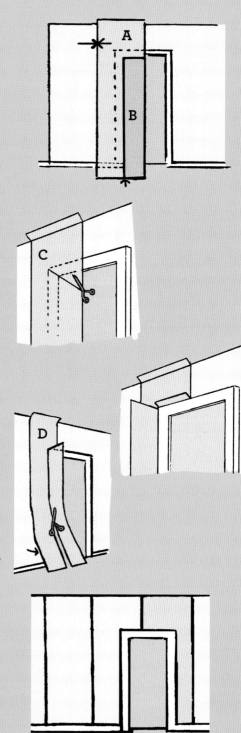

Papering around Windows

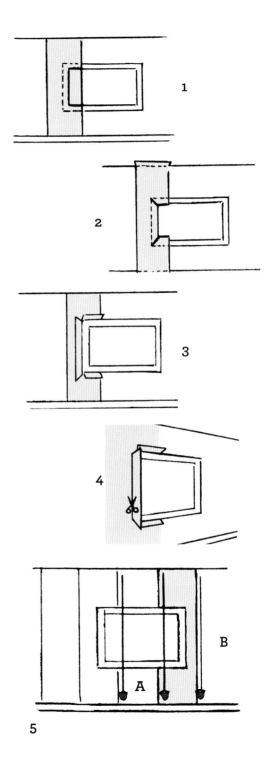

1. As with doors, hold a dry length of paper up to where it will be positioned, and mark off any area of surplus paper, shown on diagram as dark line. Cut this area off (shaded area) on the paste table.

2. Brush the paper onto the wall above and at the side of the window. Feel through the paper for the top and bottom corners of the window. Make diagonal cuts from the edge of the paper toward the window corners.

3. Brush the paper in toward the window frame so that flaps of paper are formed.

4. Score flaps where window frame meets wall using the back of the scissor points, then cut with a sharp bladed knife. **Note:** The paper at the other side of the window is dealt with in the same way.

5. In order that the paper at the far side of the window meets up and matches correctly at joint (B), it is essential that every short piece of paper above and below the window is vertically lined up. So, as each of the short lengths is hung, it is necessary to check for vertical alignment with a plumb bob at (A). Also, when hanging the length beyond the window (shaded in the diagram), it is essential to check the outer edge (B) with a plumb bob, otherwise subsequent lengths could be hung out of plumb.

Papering Windows and Doors Set Back in a Reveal

Note: Unlike windows and doors with outer frames, do not cut any surplus paper off prior to hanging.

1. Brush the paper onto the wall above the window and toward the paper joint down the side of the window (shaded area in diagram). Feel for the edge of the windowsill through the paper and make a horizontal cut along the middle of the sill's outer edge. At the end of the sill make two small angled cuts (A) toward the top and bottom of the front edge, where it meets the wall. Next, feel for the outer corner angle of the top recess, and make a horizontal cut (B) either by marking the corner lightly with a pencil then using scissors, or by using a sharp craft knife.

2. Next, turn the paper flap that the upper and lower horizontal cuts have created onto the window reveal (C). Brush up to the window frame, then where the paper meets the window frame and the windowsill, mark and cut using pencil and scissors or a sharp knife. Where the paper comes in contact with the windowsill, make an angled cut toward the front edge of the window reveal (D) and a horizontal cut along the corner where the top of the sill meets the wall (E).

3. Finally, cut off the flap below the sill and the flaps at the ceiling and baseboard. Wipe off surplus paste and brush the paper into position.

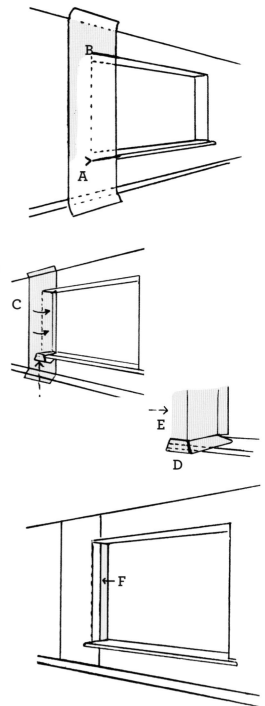

Note: Sometimes when turning paper around the reveal, it does not reach to the window frame, which leaves a narrow vertical section of bare wall (shaded area in diagram). In this case it is necessary to find a strip of matching paper and hang to edge (F).

4. The next job is to hang the short lengths of paper above and below the window making sure that the upper and lower lengths are in line vertically and plumb; use a plumb bob. When you hang the first upper length (G), there will be a small section of bare wall at the end of the upper window reveal (shaded area in diagram). It will be necessary to find an appropriately matching piece of paper for this area. Usually another small piece will be needed for the other end of the window.

5. At the other end of the window, deal with the hanging and cutting in the same way as the first reveal, except that great care has to be taken to make sure that the leading edge of the paper (H) is hanging vertically plumb, otherwise subsequent lengths could be out of plumb.

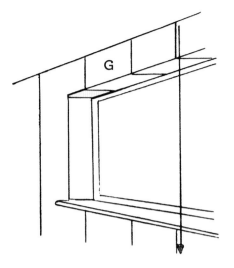

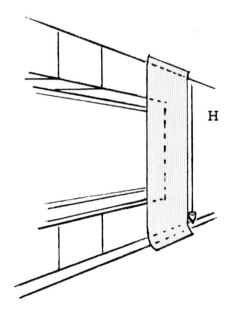

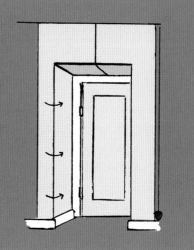

The methods of hanging described earlier for recessed windows apply to recessed doors, the only differences being that the side reveals are longer and, of course, there is no sill to worry about.

Cut along the top external corner and find small matching pieces for the upper reveal (shaded area). Plumb the leading edge of the second piece beyond the recess.

Switches and Sockets

Safety note: Turn off the electricity supply to the switch or socket.

1. Take the wallpaper loosely over the switch or socket and feel through the paper for its shape. Make a hole near the center of the switch or socket with scissor points, then make four cuts from the center hole to the corners of the switch or socket using small scissors.

2. Turn back the four triangular flaps of paper. Mark the edges of the switch or socket lightly with a pencil.

3. Lift the length of paper off the wall from the bottom, and while holding it away from the wall, cut the flaps off along the pencil marks with small scissors.

4. Brush the paper back down carefully around the switch or socket and wipe off any surplus paste.

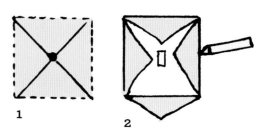

1

2

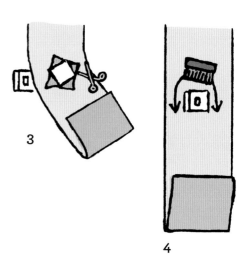

3

4

If the Switch or Socket Unscrews from the Wall

Safety note: First make sure that the electricity supply has been shut off. Unscrew the switch/socket just slightly, to leave a small gap between the switch/socket and the wall, then follow step 1 in the previous method.

Then instead of marking the edges of the switch/socket, mark a line on each paper flap about ¼ in. (5 mm) in from the edges of the switch.

Lift up the length of paper and cut off the tips of the four flaps along the pencil marks, using small pointed scissors.

Make sure that the power to the switch/socket is off as before, and tuck the four small remaining sections of paper behind the loose switch or socket with a small plastic-handled screwdriver. Then, wipe off any surplus paste and gently screw the front of the switch or socket back into place.

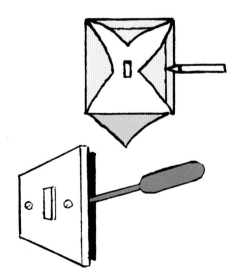

Round Obstacles, Such as Old-Fashioned Switches

As with round ceiling roses and pull switches, first make a hole near the center of the switch with the points of the scissors, then using small scissors, make a series of diagonal cuts from the center of the hole toward the outside of the switch.

Score the bottom of the created paper flaps and either cut off with a sharp craft knife or ease the length of paper off the wall and trim with small scissors.

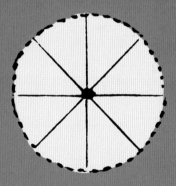

Safety note: Make sure that the electricity is turned off.

Hanging Heavyweight Papers around Switches and Sockets

Sometimes when paper is thick, it is not easy to feel the four corners of the switch or socket; in that instance it may be necessary, after making a hole in the paper near the center of the switch (A), to press the paper into the top edge of the switch/socket (B), then make two diagonal cuts from the center hole up to the two top corners of the switch (C).

Brush the paper as close to the side of the switch/socket as possible (shaded area), then feel for the bottom corner of the switch/socket and make a cut to it from the center hole (D).

Gently brush the paper as near as possible to the other side of the switch/socket (shaded area). Make a diagonal cut (E) from the center of the switch/socket to the other bottom corner of the switch/socket. Trim off the flaps of paper as described earlier. Wipe off surplus paste from switch/socket and brush down paper.

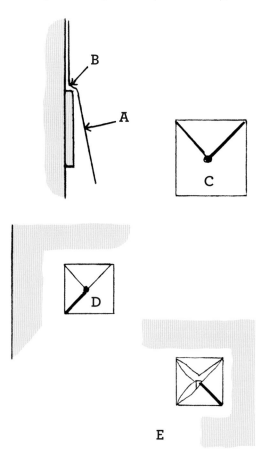

Papering around Larger Rectangular Obstacles

Service Hatches

Service hatches are treated in the same way as windows with a frame.

Length 1 is hung by making diagonal cuts to the upper and lower corners of the hatch frame.

Lengths 2 are hung above and below the hatch, with particular care being taken that the leading edges of the upper and lower lengths of paper are vertically in line and plumb.

Length 3 is hung by making diagonal cuts to the upper and lower corners of the hatch frame with particular care being taken that the leading edge of the paper is vertically plumb. Trimming is done in the same way as framed windows.

Fixed Coat Peg Boards and Handrails

Any form of long rectangular obstruction can cause problems when hanging paper. The greatest problem is keeping all the lengths above and below the obstacle vertically in line. If they are not each checked with a plumb bob, then the joint (C) of the length that goes beyond the obstacle may not match up, and the leading edge of the length can go out of plumb. The only cuts (apart from trimming) are at each end of the obstacle (A) and (B). Cut horizontally nearly toward the ends of the obstacle, then make diagonal cuts to the corners of the obstacle (A) and (B).

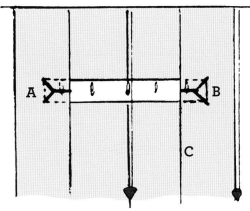

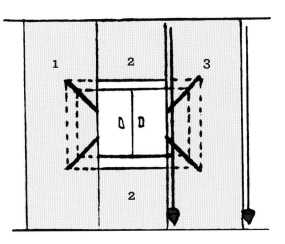

Radiators

The easiest way to deal with radiators from a decorating point of view is to get a plumber to drain and remove the radiator. If you try to do the job yourself, you may get leaks, messy carpets and possible air locks in the heating system. If removing is not an option, then it is more convenient to paper around them. If you try and push paper right down behind the radiator, it can cause wrinkling, and when papered right down, it can pose a problem when the paper needs to be stripped off at a later date. Therefore, take the paper just down below eye level at the top of the radiator, and just a little way in and out of sight at the sides.

1. Hold a dry length of paper up to where it matches the pattern with the last length of paper hung before the radiator (A). Let it drape down in front of the radiator. Mark an area with a pencil that is in from the top and side of the radiator (the solid line in the diagram). While the dry paper is held in position, feel for the top corner of the radiator (B) and make a diagonal pencil line from the corner of the radiator to the corner where the two lines meet (C).

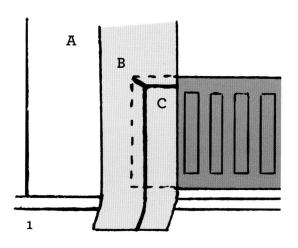

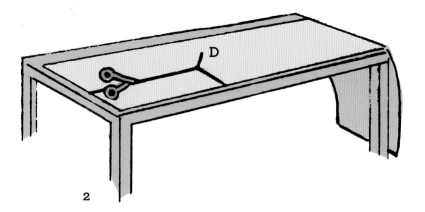

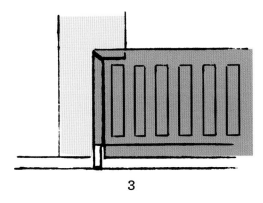

3

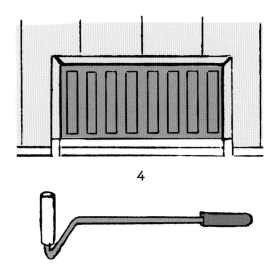

4

2. Cut off marked surplus area of the paper on the paste table and cut along the diagonal pencil lines (D). Turn over the paper. When pasting the back of the paper, a piece of scrap paper can be placed under the length where the cut out section was removed to keep the table clear of any paste.

3. Hang the length above the radiator, and tuck the top flap of paper down below the top of the radiator. Brush the paper down the side of the radiator and tuck the vertical flap of paper in behind side of radiator.

4. Hang the lengths that come over the middle area of the radiator, tucking each length about 4 in. (10 cm) down below the top edge of the radiator. **Note:** A useful tool for pushing the paper down is a wire-handled radiator roller. Finally, the length of paper at the other end of the radiator is dealt with in the same way as at the first end. Wipe off surplus paste.

Surface Pipes

If possible, try to plan the wallpaper position so that you hang from either side of the pipes, with the paper joint behind the pipe.

Another way is to remove the pipe brackets and slide the wallpaper behind the pipe, then refit the brackets by first feeling for the screw holes in the wall through the paper while it is wet.

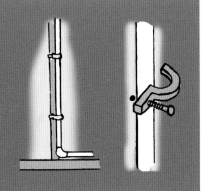

Wall Lights

The easiest way to paper around lights is to have the wall lights removed by a qualified electrician and the remaining wires safely blanked off and taped up. If this isn't possible, then try to plan the wallpapering so that a joint comes in line with the wall light, although this is not always possible—especially if there is a second wall light on the same wall.

Safety note: Always make sure that the electricity is turned off.

Another rather makeshift method I have used when the wallpaper pattern will allow it is to carefully tear along the edge of the pattern when hanging the paper. Do this toward the edge of the wall light (solid line in diagram). Tear inward from the face of the paper to minimize the effect of tearing the face of the paper. I should stress that this has to be done extremely carefully; the wallpaper can then be hung above the wall light and around it, down the opposite side of the paper to the tear. Next, the paper beneath the wall light can be hung, and the paper on either side of the tear positioned together. All that remains is to make diagonal cuts around the base of the wall light, score, and cut. This method is most suited to busy textured patterns, and does not work so well on plain, smooth papers where tears tend to show. It is easiest if the wall lights are first removed as suggested earlier.

Papering around Decorative Fireplaces

1. Before paper-hanging, it is a good idea to protect the front and sides of the fireplace with plastic held in position with masking tape. It is usual to hang wallpaper from a centerline (A) working outward toward the two outer sides of the fireplace.

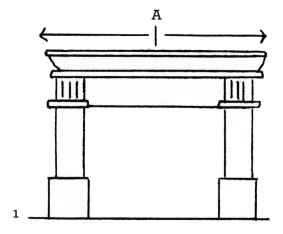

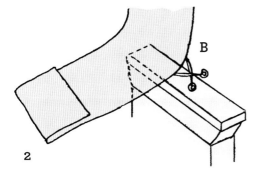

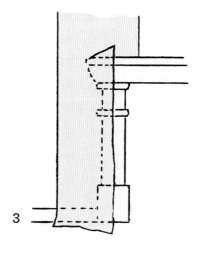

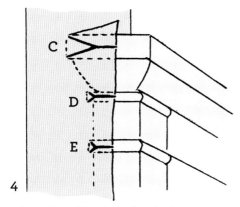

Side view of fireplace showing large vertical flap of wallpaper

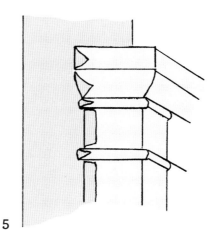

2. Hang the paper down to the top of the fireplace and mark a line where it meets the top (B). Do this along to the outer edge of the top of the fireplace. Cut just a fraction below the marked line.

3. Turn back the paper vertically, down the side of the fireplace.

4. Ease the large vertical flap of wallpaper gently up to the contours of the fireplace. Feel through the paper to where moldings project, and make diagonal cuts from the edge of the paper to these projections, see solid lines at (C), (D), and (E).

5. Cut off some of the outer surplus paper from the large vertical flap, leaving small flaps near the moldings of the fireplace. Score these around the moldings with the back of a scissor point, then either trim off the ends with a sharp craft knife, or with small scissors, keeping to the scored lines. Wipe off surplus paste before brushing the paper into position.

Hanging Borders and Creating Dado Effects

Borders come in various roll lengths and widths, but can be put in two different categories: those that are ready-pasted and those unpasted. The obvious advantage of ready-pasted is that it does not need pasting, the disadvantage being that once it is stuck in position it is firmly stuck, and it is not possible to slide it into a slightly different position or lift it back off easily. The advantage of unpasted is that it can be lifted and reapplied, or slid into a slightly different position. The disadvantage, of course, is that it requires pasting, which can be difficult as it uses long, narrow lengths of paper.

Measuring and Patterning Borders

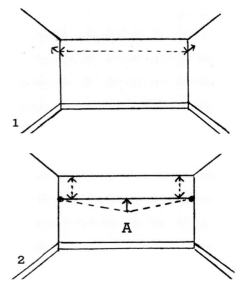

1. Measure the horizontal width of each wall, remembering to allow an extra 1 in. (25 mm) at each end for a slight lap round and patterning.
2. If you want a border hung a distance down from the ceiling, measure this distance down from the ceiling at either end of the wall. Then, using a thin chalked length of string held at either end by a large pushpin, snap a chalked line by pulling out the center of the taut string and letting it go (A).

3. Measure the length of border on the paste table; try and work it so that the same pattern comes at either end of the length. Hang the first length either up to the ceiling or at a chosen distance below, keeping the top edge of the border running along the snapped chalk line.

4. When you come to the second wall, hold the end of the dry roll of border up to the end of the first length hung, and move and fold the border until you find a horizontal match (B).

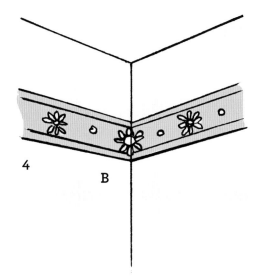

4

B

Pasting Borders

1. Place the border along the far edge of the paste table, then put weights such as scissors or ruler at either end of the border to prevent it from rolling up.

2. Use a small medium-pile roller (3 in./76 mm wide) to apply paste. Roll in one direction only at a time, not backward and forward as this would "ruck" the paper. Work toward the end of the border and outward toward the back edge of the paste table. Do not attempt to paste the inner edge of the border yet.

3. Next, pull the length of half-pasted border over to the nearside edge of the paste table, and keeping weights on either end, roll paste in one direction at a time and outward toward the nearside edge of the paste table.

4. Fold up the pasted section into concertina folds. Carry on pasting further sections of border along the paste table, and continue concertina-folding the border until you reach the end of the length.

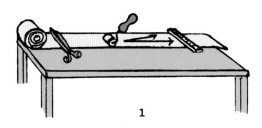

1

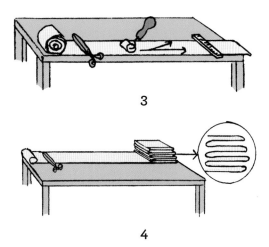

3

4

Forming Panel Effects with Borders

Sometimes a panel effect is arequired on walls (A) and occasionally on ceilings. This means that you must miter the corners where lengths of border meet at right angles.

Hang the first length (1) to where you want the corner of the panel effect to be. Then hang the second length (2) at right angles to it, letting the border overlap the first length slightly. Make a diagonal cut from the outer corner to the inner corner (3), marked in a heavy, solid line on the diagram. Using a sharp bladed knife, cut through both thicknesses of paper to leave a butt joint. Remove cut paper underneath the second length. Wipe off any surplus paste and roll down the two cut pieces with a seam roller.

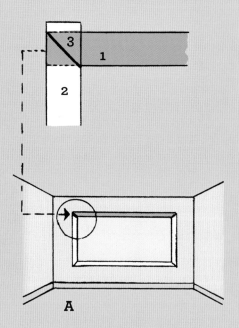

Handling and Hanging Pasted Borders

Hold the concertina folds in one hand, and let the folds out one at a time as you brush along the length of border. When you let each fold go, brush a further length of border onto the wall.

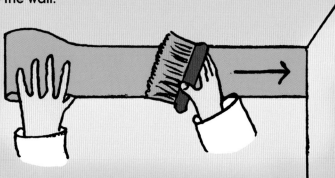

Creating Dado Effects

What is a dado? For those who do not already know, a dado is the lower section of wall, when a wall is divided into two, the upper section of wall being the largest and the lower section the smallest (A). Traditionally, the height of a dado from the skirting board to the top of the dado was approximately 3 ft. (91.5 cm).

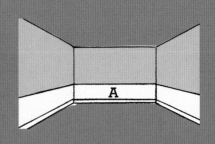

Nowadays, the height ratios may be altered. The upper and lower sections are sometimes decorated differently, and the dividing line between the two either has a wooden dado rail fitted or has a border hung along the line.

Setting Out a Dado

Note: First check that the baseboard is level horizontally using a level. If it is level, measure up from the baseboard top to the height that you want the dado to be (A and B). Make a mark at this height at either side of the wall. Fix a chalk line (thin string with chalk on it), to the marks with large pushpins, pull the string taut, then pull the string outward and let go so that the string snaps back to the wall and produces a chalk line (C).

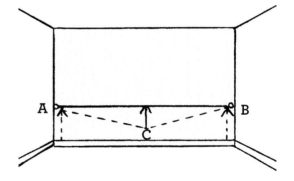

If the Baseboard Is Not Level Horizontally

Measure from the top of the baseboard to the required height of the dado and make a mark; do this at the center of the wall. Next, get a long straight lath of wood and place this up to the mark on the wall. Place a level on top of the wood (A) and move the ends of the wood

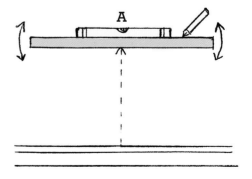

up and down slightly, keeping the middle of the wood up to the mark, until the bubble on the level indicates that the wood is placed horizontally true. Then holding the wood stationary in this position, draw a line along the top of the wood lightly with a lead pencil. Extend this line across the width of the wall and around the corners of the wall slightly onto the other walls.

Hanging Wallpaper to a Dado Line

Hang the first length into the corner of the wall so that it comes down below the marked dado line a bit—about 2 in. (5 cm) is usually enough. Place a straight edge across the paper so that the top edge is touching the marked dado line. Use the small mark on the next wall to line up the straight edge (A). Next, draw a line lightly in pencil across the paper along the top edge of the straight edge (B). Pull the paper off the wall slightly at the bottom and cut along the line with scissors. Alternatively, if the paper will allow it, cut along the straight edge with a sharp craft knife.

Carry on repeating the above and lining the straight edge up with the bottom of the previously trimmed length of paper and the marked line on the wall.

When all the upper lengths of paper are in position, hang the lower lengths. Allow a small amount (approximately 2 in./5 cm) of extra paper to come above the bottom of the upper lengths (C).

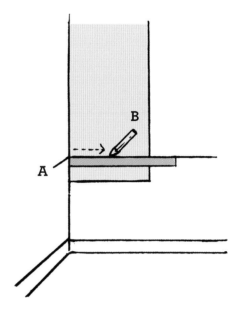

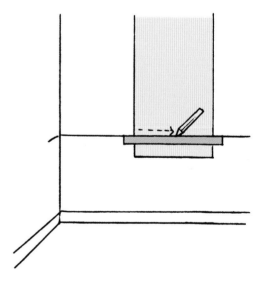

Fold this extra paper down onto the lower length (D) and cut along the fold. Carry on lining up, folding and cutting in the same way across the wall. Wipe off any surplus paste.

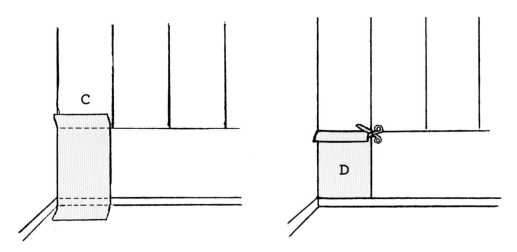

Hanging a Border to the Dado Line

Hang the border with either the top edge or the lower edge of the border (whichever you prefer) lined up with the dado line, using the same pasting and concertina-folding as described on page 150.

Note: If you hang the border with the lower edge of the border touching the dado line, it will increase the height of the dado by the width of the border.

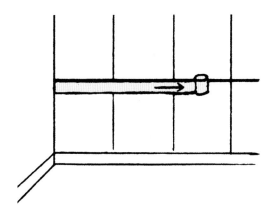

Paper-Hanging a Staircase

Getting at the work: For a straight staircase, you will need a short ladder (or a three-way ladder), a plank, and a stepladder. For a staircase that turns at the top, you will need a short ladder, two planks, and two stepladders. It is easier to use a three-way ladder in the staircase well, rather than an ordinary ladder, the top of which tends to get in the way when papering the "drop-return" wall.

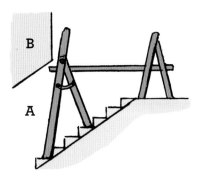

The three-way ladder (A) stands away from the drop return wall (B), thus enabling the wallpaper to be hung behind it. It also means that the three-way ladder does not have to rest on damp wallpaper.

For measuring up staircases, see page 144.

When measuring staircase drop walls, you have to add extra at the bottom of each length to allow for the angle of the "stringing" (C), the angled skirting board at the side of the stairs.

If there is an angled ceiling below the stairwell, then it is necessary to add extra length at the top (D) as well as at the bottom (E).

Sometimes people have a dado rail fitted to staircase walls; this means that longer lengths of paper aren't needed for the upper walls, but it can also mean that more paper will be required, as there will be more cutting waste. When measuring a dado area, remember to allow extra paper at the top and bottom of each length (F) and (G).

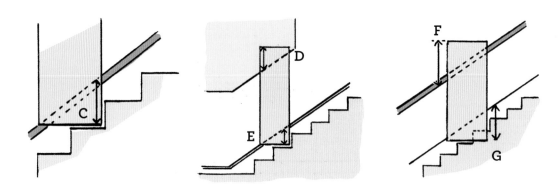

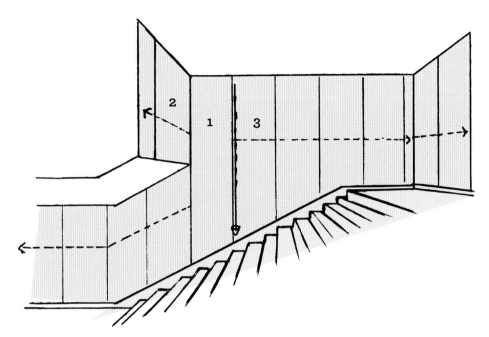

Staircase Paper-Hanging Procedures

Always start papering a stairwell with what is known as the drop length (1), then hang subsequent lengths away from it, upward toward the landing, and downward toward the hall; next hang the drop return wall (2).

Start by measuring the width of the paper and holding a plumb bob to this distance, make a series of vertical pencil marks on the wall, down the side of the plumb bob string (3).

Pasting and Folding Drop Lengths

Paste from the center of the length outward toward the edges, making a series of long concertina folds as you paste along the length of the paste table. An average drop length usually folds back into three or four long concertina folds. When you reach the far end of the length, turn a short length of paper back on itself to form a bottom fold (A).

Hanging

1. Hold the top of the concertina folds in one hand and place the beginning of the length at the top of the drop wall. Line up the leading edge of the paper with the plumbed pencil marks on the wall. When you are sure that the paper is lined up and vertically plumb, let out the remaining concertina folds, one at a time, brushing each section of paper onto the wall. As you do this, try not to swing the length sideways and check again for plumb with the plumb bob.

2. When you reach the stair "stringer" (angled baseboard) at the bottom of the length, it is a good idea to cut off the surplus paper below the stringer (solid line in diagram) before marking and trimming.

3. Next score a line with the back of the scissor points. Then, if the scored line does not show very well, mark very lightly with a pencil.

4. Lift the paper off the wall slightly from the bottom, and cut along the scored line. Wipe off surplus paste on the stringer (angled baseboard) with a damp sponge and brush the paper into place. Continue to use concertina folds for the other long lengths.

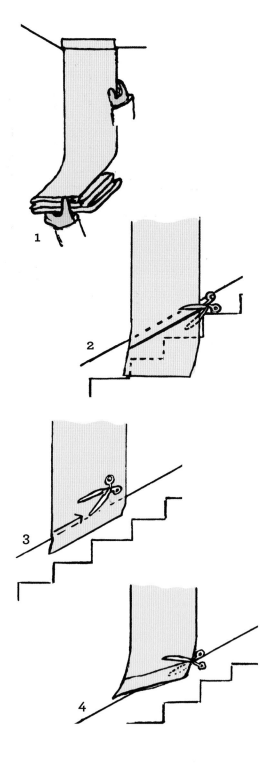

Handrails

Wherever possible, try to remove handrails prior to hanging paper. This may mean unscrewing the handrail from the metal brackets. If the brackets are left in position, they can be papered around using star-shaped cuts. If the handrail is attached to a long fixed board, then it may be necessary to paper above and below it. Cuts are made horizontally into the lengths that come at the ends of the board (see Fixed Coat Peg Boards and Handrails, page 203). Care must be taken to keep the upper and lower lengths plumb and vertically in line with each other so that the final length beyond the handrail matches up with the lengths above and below the handrail.

Paper-Hanging a Drop Return Wall (the Wall over the Stairs)

Above the stairs there is often a section of wall that has a banister rail running into it; this may be a solid panel construction, or a banister and spindles. Either way, hang the paper down as far as the top of the banister rail, and lay it on top of the rail (A). Then make a long cut from the bottom of the length toward where the banister rail meets the wall, keeping to the middle of the rail (B). At this point, make two short diagonal cuts toward the outer two top corners of the banister rail (C).

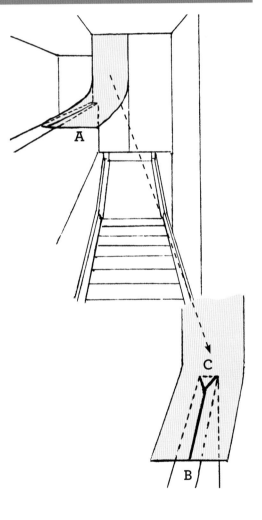

Papering around Stair Spindles

Let the two sections of paper created by the cuts fall down either side of the banisters or panels (A). If you're dealing with panels, mark down either side where the paper is in contact and cut. If they're spindles, feel for the moldings projecting on the outer edges and corners through the paper, and make a series of cuts from the cut edge of the paper beyond these to the wall (B) (solid lines on diagram). Next, press the paper gently around the contours of the spindle, score around them with the back edge of scissor points, and cut. Sometimes the spindles are set in a position away from the drop return wall. In this case, still cut along the top middle of the banister rail toward the wall. Make the same diagonal cuts to the two top corners of the rail, then mark each side of the handrail on the long vertical flaps of paper, and mark and cut horizontally just below the handrail. Complete hanging the paper by brushing the two long flaps down the wall, and carefully "butt" together the long vertical cut where the two flaps meet. Trim off the bottom and remember to wipe off any paste on the handrail or spindles.

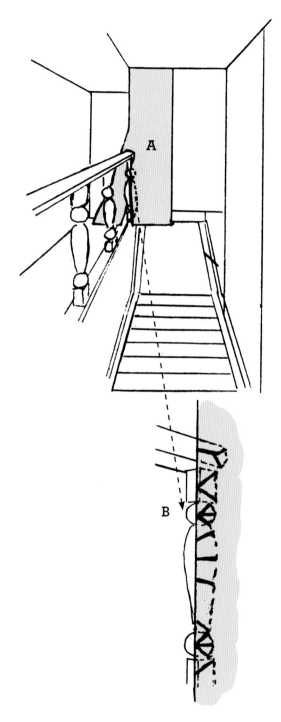

Papering a Double-Drop Wall Staircase

To use these methods it will be necessary to use a three-way ladder, adjusted so that it stands away from the wall and a plank spanning up to a stepladder on the top landing. This will allow the paper to be placed at the bottom of the drop return wall over the stairs.

Safety note: Use a craft knife with a retractable blade when working from an apron pocket and when using a ladder and a plank.

Method One

1. Start by hanging the first drop length to one of the two drop walls (side of staircase—A) as described on page 214. Hang a full width of paper to the drop return wall, above the stairs (B), matching the patterning into the corner where the two lengths meet. This leaves a section of wall (C), which is less than a width of paper. In order to keep the pattern correct at the paper joint between lengths (B) and (C) and at the corner where length (C) meets the second drop wall (D), it will be necessary to hang a full drop length from (C) around to the drop wall (D).

2. Hang the top section of the paper to the face of the drop return wall (C) over the stairs. Keep hold of the concertina folds with one hand. Make a diagonal cut near the ceiling toward the corner of the wall (E). Let the paper turn loosely around the corner and let it stick temporarily to the top of the side drop wall (D).

3. With the length of paper up out of the way, let out some of the concertina folds—enough to allow the paper to come to the bottom of the drop return wall (B). Still holding onto the remaining concertina folds with one hand, make a horizontal cut just below the bottom edge of the drop return wall (see dotted line).

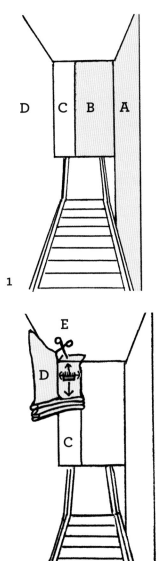

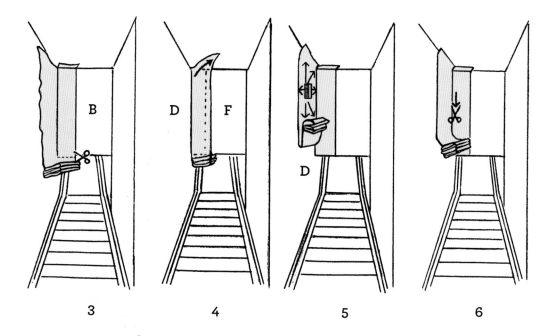

3   4   5   6

4. Pull the paper of the side drop wall (D) where it was temporarily stuck. Pull it off from the leading edge (F), still holding onto the concertina folds.

5. Carefully and lightly brush the paper so that it is temporarily stuck to the top of the sidewall (D); lightly tap the paper into the corner with the paper-hanging brush still holding onto the concertina folds with one hand.

6. Lightly score the paper into the corner of the walls with the back of the scissor points. Continue to hold onto the concertina folds with one hand.

7. Cut down the scored corner with a very sharp craft knife, or up from the bottom of the length with scissors. Continue holding the concertina folds with one hand.

8. The piece of paper on the side drop wall should now be a separate piece. Pull up the paper from the bottom until it becomes loose from the wall. Keep holding onto the concertina folds with one hand.

9. Reposition the length of paper (which is now loose) at the top of the side drop wall (D). Line up the pattern horizontally and check that the leading edge (G) is hanging vertically plumb using a plumb bob line. Keep holding the concertina folds with one hand.

10. When you are satisfied that the paper on the side drop wall (D) is hanging vertically plumb and that there is a pattern match (at last!), gently let the concertina folds drop out down the wall. Brush the paper down toward the

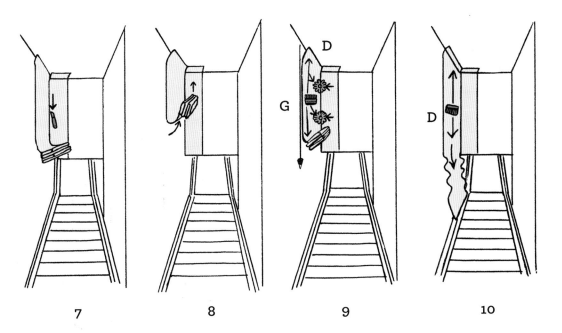

7   8   9   10

bottom of the drop return wall. Trim off the flaps of paper at the top of the walls, wipe surplus paste from the ceiling, and brush the top of the paper into position.

11. Continue brushing the paper downward. When you get to where the paper needs to go around and under the lower ceiling (hall ceiling), make a diagonal cut (H) at the corner where the return drop wall meets the lower ceiling. This will allow the paper to be positioned under the hall ceiling. Brush the paper up to the hall ceiling and score where it meets with the points of the scissors. Pull the paper off slightly and cut along the scored line. Wipe surplus paste off the lower ceiling and brush the paper into position. Finally, brush the paper down to the stair stringer (angled baseboard). Wipe off any surplus paste, then brush the paper into position.

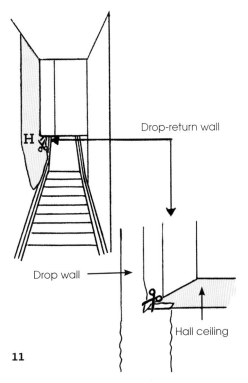

Drop-return wall

Drop wall

Hall ceiling

11

Method Two (Alternative Method of Hanging Wallpaper to a Double-Drop Wall Staircase)

This second method may appear easier than the last one, but in some respects it can be more difficult because it relies on really accurate measurements.

1. Having hung the long drop length to the first drop wall (A) and the width of paper to the drop return wall (B) (over the stairs), slightly unroll a dry roll of paper and hold it up next to the length of paper hung on the drop return wall. Move it up and down until the pattern aligns between the two.

2. Either mark with a pencil or nick the paper where the top of the roll meets the ceiling (C).

3. Having placed the roll on the paste table, measure the walls accurately: the distance (height) between the ceiling and just below the bottom of the drop return wall (above the stairs). Also, measure the width from the leading edge of the paper hung on the drop return wall and the corner (D) where it meets the other long drop wall.

Note: It is a good idea to measure this width at more than one position, as the corner of the walls may vary. Use the widest measurement. Then measure the total height of the long side drop wall from the ceiling down to the stair stringer (E) (angled baseboard).

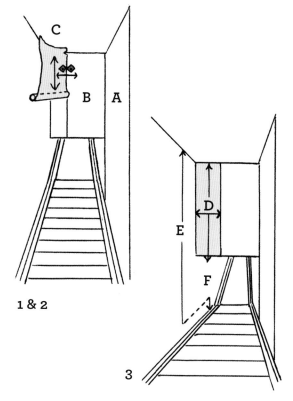

1 & 2

3

Remember: When measuring to the stair stringer, measure further down the wall below the hall ceiling (F) as you will need extra length of paper when the long drop length goes under the hall ceiling.

4. Measure the total wall height measurement along the roll of paper; do this along the paste table.

5. Using the marking method as described on page 158, mark the width measurement and the return drop wall height measurement onto the top section of the long cut length of paper (marking the back of the paper is the most convenient).

Note: Make sure that the marking is from the correct paper edge.

6. Either paste the marked length of paper and cut the marked lines wet, which leaves two pasted lengths of paper, OR cut out the marked area of paper, which leaves a short length of paper for above the stairs (drop return wall), and a long "L"-shaped length of paper for the long drop wall. The "L" shape at the bottom of the length will go under the hall ceiling. If the paper has been cut dry, paste and hang the lengths described separately, patterning in the corner and plumbing the long drop length vertically.

Method Three (The Easier Alternative to Methods One and Two)

A way to avoid the rather difficult methods described earlier is to choose a plain paper or one that has no pattern repeat, such as an all-over pattern or a textured paper. Hang the first long drop length (A) and the full- and part-width of paper to the drop return wall (B) (over the stairs), followed by hanging a second full drop length (C) to the second long drop wall, hanging the paper from the corner. Check that the leading edge of the paper is hanging vertically plumb with a plumb bob and line.

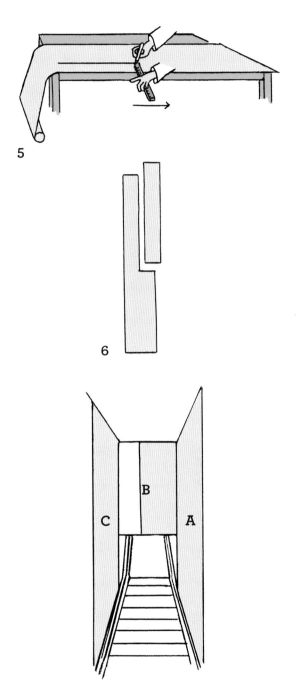

5

6

Cleaning Up Wallpapering Tools

At the end of a decorating job, it is necessary to clean the tools and equipment used.

- Wipe the edges of the paste table with a damp sponge.

- Wash the paper-hanging brush and the seam roller with warm water and liquid soap (washing-up liquid is useful). Make sure that the bristles of the paper-hanging brush are thoroughly dry before storing the brush in a box or bag.

- Clean the scissor blades with water and rub with a plastic scouring pad.

- Scrape out the paste brush or roller into the paste bucket. To clean the roller, use the side of a knife blade to scrape out most of the thick paste from the roller sleeve. Wash out the roller (or brush) with hot water and liquid soap, then dry with rags or shake out the brush and leave to dry.

- Dispose of any mixed paste left over by diluting it with plenty of hot water. Stir well until the paste disperses into the hot water, then flush down a toilet. It may be necessary to repeat this.

Wallpapering Problems and Remedies

Wrinkles

Causes

- Stretching the paper by overbrushing.

Remedies

- There is no real remedy except stripping off the paper and starting again.

Loose Joints and/or Paper Coming Away from the Surface

Causes

- The edges of the wallpaper have been missed when pasting, resulting in dry seams.
- When a vinyl paper is overlapped slightly onto another length of vinyl (vinyl does not stick well to vinyl, unless an overlap adhesive is used).
- Soft distemper-like paint has come away from the wall on the back of the paper, due to insufficient preparation of the surface.
- Paste was not mixed to a strong enough consistency.
- Paper coming away from a gloss-painted surface that was not flatted down prior to hanging the paper.
- Excessive heat, which can dry out the adhesive and paper.
- Misses when pasting, resulting in uneven paper soakage.

Remedies

- Make sure that the surfaces are thoroughly prepared prior to hanging paper.
- Flaking paint surfaces should be scraped, sanded, filled, and fastened down with a primer sealer or diluted PVA adhesive.
- Powdery paint surfaces, such as distemper, should be washed off wherever possible. Porous surfaces should always be either sealed, or have a "size coat" applied. Gloss-painted surfaces should be well flatted down, not size coated, and a lining paper hung before wallpapering.
- Be thorough when pasting, and make sure that the paper toward the edges is coated.
- Avoid overlapping joints, especially when hanging vinyl papers.
- Always follow the paste manufactures instructions when mixing paste.
- Use a seam roller, except on delicate papers and hollow-backed textures.

Remedial treatment (where possible) Lift loose joints, apply overlap adhesive and roll down.

Blisters
Causes

- Loose paint coming away on the back of the paper.
- Not enough soakage time allowed for the paper.

Remedies

- When blisters occur after hanging, leave for an hour or two; many blisters will "tighten back" as the paper dries.
- If the blisters do not tighten back, try pricking a hole in them with a pin, then rolling down. If this does not work, open them up using a very sharp craft knife. Make cuts from the center of the blister toward the edges. Next, turn back the four triangular paper flaps you have created. Carefully remove any loose paint (distemper, etc.) from the back of

the flaps and from the exposed surface. Apply overlap adhesive to the back of the flaps and the surface. Make sure that the flaps are soaked and pliable before rolling down into position with a seam roller. Remove surplus paste.

Shiny Joints ("Burnishing")

Causes

- Overbrushing or too much rolling with a seam roller.

Note: Matte-finished papers ar particularly susceptible to burnishing.

Remedies

- Careful and systematic brushing, and the minimum of rolling on delicate papers.
- Very carefully wash the surface of the paper, but this does not always work.

White or "Milky" Patches on the Face of the Paper

Causes

- Paste on the face of the paper.

Remedies

- Careful application of the paste; keep the paste table clean.
- When hanging the paper, avoid letting the length catch the face of the previously hung length.
- Always wipe off any paste on the face of the paper immediately with a damp sponge.
- If the paper will stand it, wash the face with warm water and a small amount of liquid soap; dry off thoroughly.

Shrink Back of Joints

Causes

- The paper literally shrinks on drying, exposing the surface between the joints, especially when the paper has been hung over loose powdery surfaces, such as distemper.
- Hung on top of a nonporous surface, such as gloss paint.
- Incorrect soakage time can cause shrink back.
- Exposure of the paper to heat (too rapid dry out).

Remedies

- Thorough preparation of surfaces.
- Correct soakage time.
- Turning heat sources off near newly papered surfaces.
- Using lining paper underneath the wallpaper.

Remedial suggestion Try finding a colored pencil or crayon that resembles the color of the paper, and carefully fill in the gaps between the joints with color. Other than that, little can be done except to strip off the paper and rehang.

Index

Photo Credits

page 72: Coprid; foxie page 73: foxie; P-fotography page 74: topseller; Taiga page 75: Anteromite page 76: foxie page 77: Lustrator; Juriah Mosin page 79: Fotokostic page 80: Cultura Motion page 82: Perseo Studio page 83: foxie page 85: Manuel Trinidad Mesa page 87: Stacey Newman page 88: Sergey Ryzhov page 89: Phovoir; Suwatchai Pluemruetai page 90: Suwatchai Pluemruetai page 91: foxie page 93: Phovoir page 97: Benoit Daoust page 99: foxie page 101: stockphoto-graf; Lustrator; Ingvald Kaldhussater page 102: Serenethos page 104: Gunter Kremer page 105: tdhster page 106: Lustrator page 109: McElroy Art page 111: Marc Dietrich page 112: foxie page 113: Ashley van Dyck; Andreey page 114: Epitavi; Mario7 page 115: tphatrapornnant page 116: Laurentlesax; Milosz_G page 117: anndypit; severija pages 118–119: goir; Yunava1 pages 120–121: Thomas Holt page 122: Kameel4u page 123: Rob van Hal; Lustrator page 124: foxie page 125: Dn Br pages 126–127: goodluz page 128: foxie page 129: Photographee.eu page 130: Hayati Kayhan page 131: purplequeue page 132: foxie page 133: Lustrator page 134: ronstik page 135: foxie page 137: vvoe; foxie page 138: Lolostock page 139: foxie page 140: ronstik; Lustrator page 141: nadisja page 142: fotogenicstudio; Lustrator page 144: foxie page 146: Dar1930 page 147: vipman page 148: Lustrator; Dar1930 page 151: Yunava1 page 152: foxie page 153: Dmitry Kalinovsky; Gavran333; Panyawatt; AlexKZ; UVgreen; stockphoto-graf; Studio DMM Photography, Designs & Art; Sangaroon Sungkomsilp; agolndr; Phovoir; Jr images; Mega Pixel; goir; Steve Cukrov page 154: SpeedKingz; page 160: foxie page 161: Mr Twister page 165: Phovoir page 166: Suwatchai Pluemruetai page 168: vdimage page 179: Lustrator; SpeedKingz pages 180, 181: foxie page 183: Phovoir page 187: fotogenicstudio page 188: Phovoir page 190: foxie; Denizo71 page 192: foxie page 193: fotogenicstudio page 194: Dar1930 page 196: foxie page 202: sirtravelalot page 208: Phovoir page 224: Alex_Po page 225: Twin Design page 226: jjspring page 227: Evgeniia Trushkova; MicrostockStudio page 229: scelap page 233: sirtravelalot

About the Author

Born in Yorkshire, England, Michael Light attended night school while serving a six-year apprenticeship to a firm of decorators in Harrogate, Yorkshire. He won a scholarship to an art and technical college and would go on to earn certificates from the City & Guild of London, as well as Fellow of the Institute of British Decorators and Interior Designers. With over forty years of professional trade experience, he has taught decorating and has run his own successful business.